A Teachers' Guide to
Action Research

A Teachers' Guide to Action Research

*Evaluation, Enquiry and
Development in the Classroom*

Edited by JON NIXON

GRANT
MCINTYRE

First published in 1981 by
Grant McIntyre Ltd
39 Great Russell Street
London WC1B 3PH

British Library Cataloguing in Publication Data
A teachers' guide to action research
  1. Action research   2. Teaching – Research
  I. Nixon, Jon
  371.10207'2   H62

  ISBN 0-86216-040-5
  ISBN 0-86216-041-3 Pbk

Text set in 10/12 pt Linotron 202 Bembo, printed and bound in Great Britain at
The Pitman Press, Bath

Contents

JOHN ELLIOTT

Foreword

This book represents another landmark in the history of the 'teachers as researchers' movement. It marks the gradual development over the last twelve years of an alternative educational research community which is based in the schools rather than Institutes of Higher Education. This does not mean that the movement necessarily excludes researchers from the higher education sector. But it insists that the value of their contributions lies in the extent to which they support the practical judgment of teachers, and increase their capacity to reflect systematically upon the complex situations they confront. The identification of problems for investigation, the methods of research employed, and the presentation of 'findings' will all be executed through negotiation and collaboration with teachers. However, the future prosperity of the movement will increasingly depend on teachers grasping opportunities to conduct their own enquiries without external support.

Whether teacher-based research operates autonomously or collaboratively it marks a radical departure from the traditional view of educational research as a specialist activity, the results of which teachers apply rather than create. The truth is that teachers have consistently failed to see how the abstract generalisations of traditional empirical research apply to the concrete and complex situations in which they have to operate. The teacher as researcher movement, with its focus on the practical educational problems arising from particular situations, and with its aim of illuminating such situations for those involved, offers an alternative solution to the familiar 'applicability of findings' issue.

It is my belief that the teacher as researcher movement in the United Kingdom can be traced to the formative influence of one

man, Lawrence Stenhouse. It is no accident that the majority of
teachers brought together by Jon Nixon have nearly all at
sometime been either directly or indirectly connected with a
Stenhouse enterprise.

Some authors in this book refer to their experience as teacher-
researchers on projects directed by Stenhouse. The first of these,
which began in 1967, was the Schools Council's Humanities
Curriculum Project. Although HCP produced materials, it was
basically concerned with helping teachers to explore the effects
of implementing a radical new pedagogy for the study of
controversial issues in classrooms. One of the important outcomes of HCP was the first teacher as researcher book, *People in
Classrooms*, edited by myself and Barry MacDonald (see Appendix). This book consisted of a series of case studies which
explored the problems of implementing 'the neutral teacher' role
and its effects on pupils. Also cited in the following pages are the
MACOS and 'Teaching about Race Relations' Projects. Stenhouse co-ordinated the dissemination of the former in the
United Kingdom, and initiated the latter as a result of the
Schools Council's refusal to support the idea of 'the neutral
teacher' when handling 'race issues'. Jon Nixon was himself
involved in the teacher-based action research programme on
which much of the 'Race Relations' project was based.

Another Stenhouse-inspired successor to the Humanities Project was the Ford Teaching Project, which I, formerly a member
of the HCP team, directed. This project involved forty East
Anglian teachers in an enquiry into the problems of implementing enquiry-discovery methods across the curriculum.
Over twenty monographs and case studies, many written by the
teachers themselves, flowed from this project. One of the
contributors to this book, David Ebbutt, was a prominent
teacher-researcher on the Ford Project, the materials of which
formed the basis of a series of dissemination conferences from
1974 to 1976. The majority who attended were lecturers from
higher education; little interest was apparent at the grass-roots.
But as the 1970s drew to a close grass-roots interest developed,
stimulated by LEA Advisers and Teachers' Centre Wardens,
some of whom had attended the dissemination conferences. One

adviser who came was the late Fred Baker from Bedfordshire. Subsequently, Fred began to encourage teacher-based research and evaluation in Luton schools. Nigel Rumble, a contributor to this book and currently Head of Science at Halyard School, was one teacher who came into contact with the teacher as researcher movement through Fred Baker. On his appointment as Warden of Watford Teachers' Centre, Ray Shostak came into contact with the publications of Ford T, which moved its base with me from UEA to the Cambridge Institute of Education in 1976. Subsequently Ray Shostak established local teacher-researcher groups supported from his Watford Centre.

In 1976 the Classroom Action Research Network was established and co-ordinated from the Cambridge Institute. Supported originally by a grant from the Ford Foundation, it aimed to strengthen the links between emerging teacher-based research groups. Through its annual Bulletin, CARN disseminates the ideas and reports of such groups, in addition to those of the lone teacher-researcher. The network also embraces people interested in teacher-based research in Europe, the USA and Canada, Australia and New Zealand. Through the network Ray Verrier and Jon Nixon contacted each other and embarked on collaborative action-research together.

Every year, beginning in 1978, CARN has held an Annual Conference. The teachers present at past conferences, somewhat outnumbered by higher education representatives talking research methodology, tended to feel 'outsiders'. In 1979, Jon Nixon decided it was time to gather a group of teacher-researchers together, apart from academics like me. He achieved his aim with the help of a grant from the Schools Council, who subsequently published a short conference report. Amongst the very few academics in attendance were Ray Verrier and Gail McCutcheon, both of whom had previously attended the first (and very successful) CARN Conference in 1978. Some of the teachers involved in both conferences made a major contribution to the 1980 national CARN Conference.

At this Conference access was restricted to those teachers able to bring evidence they had collected from their own classrooms, and to those 'academics' actively conducting collaborative research with teachers. Beginning with small group analyses of the evidence presented, the teachers present, assisted by consultants, planned individual and group research projects to be carried out during 1980/81 and presented at the 1981 conference.

Gradually, accounts of teacher-based research are being written-up, shared, and made accessible. The teacher as researcher movement is evolving 'naturally' in response to the perceived needs of teachers; a lightly steered movement rather than a heavily controlled formal organisation. The latter would probably stifle the free information flow so necessary to the continual development of ideas which all teachers can contribute and have access to. Organisations spawn permanent 'control' centres. Within movements and networks initiative and leadership constantly shift. Without one such shift this book would never have emerged, and I would not have been elevated to the status of the 'grand old man' who writes 'the foreword'.

John Elliott
Cambridge Institute of Education
November 1980

JON NIXON

Introduction

What is educational research? Disputation on irrelevant issues in impossibly esoteric journals? The testing of unworkable materials foisted upon schools by ivory-tower academics whose first-hand knowledge of the classroom is at best out-of-date and at worst non-existent? Eye-catching reports which, with the help of the popular press, tarnish the reputation of creative, experimental teaching?

For many the answer to these questions will be an unqualified 'yes': much educational research, both in principle and practice, remains an activity indulged in by those *outside* the classroom for the benefit of those *outside* the classroom. Teachers, if they are considered at all, are seen merely as the consumers, never as the producers, of original research. This guide offers an alternative in the form of action research conducted by teachers for teachers. The research reported in the following pages was initiated, conducted and disseminated *from the inside*. It represents a tradition of systematic enquiry, by means of which teachers are able to communicate to colleagues and other interested parties insights culled from their classrooms, and to use these insights in such a way as to improve their own teaching.

This tradition is in no way exclusive. One of the assumptions underlying this guide is that action research can be undertaken by any teacher in any classroom. This is not to say, however, that it can be undertaken lightly. Action research is an intellectually demanding mode of enquiry, which prompts serious and often uncomfortable questions about classroom practice. It requires a willingness on the part of teachers to learn about their own classrooms and a desire to develop themselves professionally. The teacher who engages in action research is not a special kind of teacher, but simply one who wishes to increase his or her professional expertise.

The case for action research may be stated briefly. By investigating and reflecting upon their own practice teachers may increase their understanding of the classroom. Understanding why a particular child is upset or withdrawn may not imply a different course of action on the teacher's part, but it does help the teacher make sense of that child's behaviour. The development of this kind of understanding may well be seriously undervalued within a policitical and economic climate such as ours, which seems to foster increasingly instrumentalist policies and short-term planning.

In other cases, however, the understanding derived from action research may be acted upon. For it informs the teacher's judgment about such things as how children learn, what the critical moments in this learning process are, and how and when the teacher should intervene so as to facilitate this process. These kinds of enquiry may increase the knowledge and understanding of teachers in such a way that they are able to respond more sensitively to the needs of their pupils in terms of both face to face classroom interactions and more formal aspects of curriculum planning and school organisation.

In addition to increasing the understanding and informing the decisions of teachers, action research may also bring about a modification or elaboration of theories of teaching and learning. Research, in this respect at least, may be seen as an ongoing professional duty. It makes explicit the teaching acts; it informs them and enables the practitioner to understand the context within which they are embedded.

Clearly, this book cannot address the particular problems of every classroom teacher. It is important, therefore, that in working through the following chapters readers should retain a clear sense of their own specific wants and needs. Help may be needed, for example, in planning and conducting action research with an examination class or in the context of modern languages teaching. Although this book does not specifically tackle either of these two issues, the cases it reports contain ideas and suggestions which would be of help to all teachers regardless of the age-group they teach or of their subject specialism. In designing an action research project, however grand or modest the scale, it is essential that teachers should start from where they are.

That is precisely what those whose work is reported in this book have done. They have started from their own skills and inclinations and from their own enthusiasms. Very few of them had received any training in research methods, although in a few cases the research was carried out as part of a higher degree course. Each of them began from a simple desire to learn, and progressed, sometimes by hints and guesses, towards the development of a research style which suited their own particular needs and circumstances. The teacher whose initial training has been in the humanities is likely to engage in a very different style of research from the teacher with a scientific training. But each is capable of generating new and exciting insights. Action research is nothing if not eclectic.

This eclecticism may prove to be a stumbling block to the reader who has too narrow a view of educational research. A conscious effort should be made to bracket any preconceived ideas concerning the correctness or otherwise of a particular research model. What matters is the extent to which the model is appropriate; appropriate to the skills of the teacher, the constraints of the classroom and the nature of the problem to be explored. The single most important point to be taken from this book is the necessity of developing one's own unique way of looking at those complex environments in which pupils are constrained, and teachers choose, to spend their working lives.

It is for precisely this reason that the present volume is described as 'a guide'. The following reports of research activities aspire to give to those working in classrooms a sense of direction without a sense of being directed. Many of the contributors, as they would be the first to admit, have learnt a great deal from one another; confirming new insights, discussing tapes and transcripts, observing lessons. They also learnt from numerous other colleagues whose work is not represented here. The publication of this book is an attempt to widen the scope of the collaborative venture. The ideas it contains should be tested against the reader's own experience of the classroom. Only insofar as they are tried out, modified and criticised by other practitioners working in schools can these ideas further the development of a research tradition which has its feet on the ground and its heart in the classroom.

The task of developing a research tradition of this kind cannot be achieved by a single individual, or even a small group. It is an enterprise which needs to be discussed and shared. The most effective way of reading this book would be within study groups based within schools and teachers' centres. While a single teacher attempting to adopt a research stance within a school is likely to face at the very least a sense of isolation, a group of teachers can give one another invaluable support, both moral and practical. The temptation to go it alone is considerable, but it is a temptation which should be resisted. For the quality of the research may ultimately depend to a very large extent on the collaborative relationship which sustains it.

The attempt throughout is to explore the role of the teacher as researcher within a number of different settings – the classroom, the school and the wider educational context – so as to further the task of developing an effective methodology of classroom research. In the first section a number of research reports have been selected which serve as examples of the various ways of doing research in the classroom. The second section sets action research in its social context with four pieces which explore some of the problems of implementing school-based research and outline possible strategies for overcoming the organisational constraints imposed by the school. Finally, members of three outside agencies describe how they have tried to offer support to teachers engaged in classroom research. Concluding this third section is a piece by the one contributor to the volume who works outside the British educational system. Gail McCutcheon, who worked for eight years in American schools before moving into higher education, assesses the unique contribution that teachers might make to our knowledge about schooling. This last chapter is the only one written by a professional research worker and represents, within the structure of the book, a significant widening of the area of debate:

between, on the one hand, the teaching profession in schools and, on the other, the university-based academic research community; and also between those concerned with teacher-initiated action research on both sides of the Atlantic. Some of the implications of this widening debate form the basis of my own Postscript.

One thing ought to be emphasised here. For many teachers the initial enthusiasm for classroom research is prompted by a desire to find more effective ways of assessing pupils' progress, diagnosing learning difficulties and analysing examination results. This book does not set out to tackle these problems directly. In so far as action research improves teaching it also improves the quality of the learning within the classroom. Those who approach this book in search of a primer on pupil assessment will, however, be disappointed. Action research serves primarily to sharpen perceptions, stimulate discussion and encourage questioning. As such it involves teachers in assessing themselves as well as their pupils.

If the teaching profession is to reject the paternalism of traditional research within education, it must develop a radical alternative which truly serves the needs of teachers. Action research as practised by the contributors to this volume and by teachers in countless classrooms represents just such an alternative. For it enables them to take a major role in developing the lines of educational enquiry, and thereby to make a unique contribution to our understanding of what happens in classrooms.

1

Classroom concerns

JON NIXON

Classroom concerns

There is no single way of doing research in the classroom. The methods employed will depend to a large extent on the skills of the teacher, the nature of the research problem and the resources available. The four pieces of research reported in this section represent a variety of approaches adopted in very different situations by teachers with diverse skills and aptitudes. One teacher tracked the development of a pupil's painting of landscape; another kept a detailed diary of what had happened in her classroom over two half-term periods; and a third was concerned with monitoring the views of his pupils on a particular unit of work. The final contributor to this section describes how tests were devised to ascertain pupils' understanding of certain concepts used in science. Each of the methods proved useful given the classroom in which it was employed and the purposes for which it was intended. No two classrooms, though, are ever alike. The following reports should be seen, therefore, not as tramlines to be followed obsessively, but as guidelines to help teachers develop a research style of their own. The key question is: what works best for me in my particular classroom with this particular group of pupils? In order to answer that question teachers need first to assess their particular skills, the constraints of the situation in which they are working, and the nature of the problem to be explored.

1. All teachers possess certain skills which can contribute to the research task. The important thing is to clarify and define one's own particular set of skills. Some teachers, for example, are able to collect and interpret statistical data; others to record in retrospective accounts the key moments of a lesson. One teacher may know something about

questionnaire design; another have a natural flair for interviewing. It is essential that teachers work from their own
particular strengths when developing the research.

2. The situations within which teachers work impose different
   kinds of constraints. Some schools, for example, are equip-
   ped with the most up-to-date audio-visual equipment,
   others cannot even boast a cassette tape recorder. Some
   have spare rooms in which interviews could be carried out,
   others hardly have enough space to implement the existing
   timetable. Action research must be designed in such a way
   as to be easily implemented within the pattern of constraints existing in the school.

3. Any initial definition of the research problem will almost
   certainly be modified as the research proceeds. Nevertheless, this definition is important because it helps to set limits
   to the enquiry. If, for example, a teacher sets out to explore
   through action research the problem of how to start a
   lesson effectively, the research will tend to focus upon the
   first few minutes of the lesson. The question of what data
   to collect is very largely answered by a clear definition of
   the research problem.

MICHAEL ARMSTRONG

The case of Louise and the painting of landscape

How are we to understand the growth of understanding? Most attempts by students of human development have been made outside the classroom, in laboratories and clinics, or in the studies and libraries of universities and research institutes. Or if research has taken place within classrooms, it has been conducted by outsiders who have played little part in the daily life of the class, least of all in teaching. Participant observers have not, for the most part, been observant participators. It is commonly assumed that the requirements of objectivity oblige us to eliminate teaching from the list of serviceable research techniques. The unfortunate consequence is that we thus deprive ourselves of a powerful, if rarely articulated, source of evidence and insight as to the nature of intellectual growth. For part of the art of teaching consists in eliciting, analysing and seeking to make more reflective the thought and action of others: consists, that is to say, in asking children questions, discussing their ideas, exchanging experience with them, finding out what they know and how they think, watching them grow. There is a self-consciousness implicit in this aspect of a teacher's activity that makes those teachers who manage it successfully – however fitful and fragmentary their success – students of those they teach as well as their teachers. Participant observation is characteristic of their method and inseparable from it.

The kind of enquiry – critical but not necessarily scientific – which I want to illustrate in this article takes the teacher's professional interest in studying children as its starting point. At the most general level the purpose of the enquiry is to enhance our understanding of intellectual growth and its enabling conditions. To this end it seeks to capitalise on teachers' diagnostic and analytical skills by providing them with an opportunity to achieve a greater detachment, a closer scrutiny, and a more precise speculation in their observation of their pupils' thought and action than their circumstances generally permit. For even where a school's curriculum, method and organisation are sufficiently flexible to allow teachers to be responsive to, and respectful of, their pupils' individual interests, habits of thought and working methods, the pressures of time, space and numbers tend to frustrate their best intentions. In classes of thirty or more children, the task of studying those we teach, however urgent, is exceptionally difficult; many teachers, and I dare say most researchers, would claim that it is frankly impossible.

In the autumn of 1976 I began an enquiry which sought to ease this task by reducing the daily pressures of teaching, thereby opening the way for teachers to devote more of their time and energy to sustained observation. In essence the strategy was simple: to allocate two teachers to a single class of children, with joint, though not necessarily equal, responsibility, for teaching and research. In pursuit of this strategy I was given leave of absence from the secondary school in which I was teaching at the time to spend a year as teacher and observer in a primary school classroom elsewhere within the same local authority. Three factors conditioned my choice of school. I wanted to work with a class which had a single regular teacher rather than a succession of teachers for each separate part of the curriculum. Effectively this meant working in a primary school. I wanted, also, to work in a school which was at least relatively informal in its methods, allowing its pupils some degree of self-determination in their learning. This seemed to me to be a necessary pre-condition for observing the course of learning and of growth. Lastly, I wanted to work with a teacher who was as interested in helping me to observe the class as I was in helping to teach it.

With the aid of friends and of the senior primary school adviser, I managed to find a school which satisfied each of the three conditions, a small town primary school of five hundred children between the ages of five and eleven. There I worked throughout the school year of 1976/77, spending all but a few weeks of my time with one teacher, Stephen Rowland, in his class of thirty-two 8 to 9 year old children: 'second year juniors'. Our aim, as I have indicated, was to teach the children on the one hand, while on the other hand observing, analysing and describing, as closely and carefully as we could, the character of their learning. The pattern of our collaboration was, briefly, as follows. During the school day I taught alongside Stephen and under his general direction. Occasionally I had charge of the whole class by myself, or of some part of it, but most of the time I moved around the classroom freely, working with children in ones, twos or threes, as occasion demanded. Although we never drew a clear distinction between our respective roles within the classroom, the children were in no doubt as to the difference between us: Stephen was their 'proper teacher', I was his 'helper'. At the end of each day we would talk things over, rehearsing the day's events and exchanging ideas about how the children were learning. In the evenings, instead of preparing, assessing and recording the children's work as Stephen had to, I would write about the day. In these field notes, the heart of our enquiry, I tried to record in some detail what seemed to me, on reflection, to be the most significant events of the day, together with my observations, interpretations and speculations about them. Sometimes I wrote down everything I could recall about the day; more often I chose to discuss particular incidents, children, or pieces of work – whatever seemed to bear most directly on the character of the children's learning. These notes were subjective inasmuch as they recorded my own judgments and impressions, but I tried hard to guard against my own prejudices and I continually checked my impressions against those of Stephen and of other observers of our classroom. Every week Stephen read through my notes, adding comments on interleaved pages. I tried to incorporate into the notes the ideas and impressions which we had exchanged in conversation during the day. Well before the end of the school year, the daily notes had begun to represent not so much my own personal viewpoint as a shared judgment, elaborated in our seemingly endless conversations. Stephen wrote notes of his own, too, usually once or twice a fortnight, concentrating on incidents in which I had not been so directly involved. We also showed what we had written to the head teacher of the school; her comments and observations, besides exposing many a superficial judgment in the notes, often helped us to identify particular lines of enquiry worth examining more closely. By the end of the year I had written all told some three hundred thousand words while Stephen and the headteacher between them had contributed a further thirty thousand or so. We had also assembled a large quantity of the children's 'products' – writings, paintings, models, charts and such like – for further analysis. It was from these notes, the conversations out of which they grew and to which they led, and the samples of work assembled in support of their descriptive analyses, that the central themes of our enquiry began to emerge.

In studying the thought and action of the children in Stephen Rowland's class I had chosen, almost from the start, to concentrate my attention on moments of intellectual absorption: those occasions on which the children were more or less evidently engrossed in their work, whether it was a matter of writing, painting, calculating, experimenting, constructing, speculating, or whatever. Such occasions seem likely to be of critical importance, both in the course of learning itself and in thinking about the course of learning. It is not, in my view, in their unguarded moments, but in their moments of absorption, when they are most in earnest and yet often, also, most playful, that children reveal most about the quality of their thought and the character of their development. The more closely Stephen and I studied the varied absorptions of the children in our own class the more impressed we were by the evidence of their appropriative skill, whether as writers or artists, scientists or inventors, however primitive their technique or limited their understanding. It seemed to us that from their earliest acquaintance with the various traditions of human thought – literature, art, science, mathematics – our pupils were engaged in a continual struggle, by turns satisfying and frustrating, to make use of whatever limited knowledge, skill and experience they possessed to examine, extend and express in an appropriate form their own particular understanding of the world in which they lived, 'to reproduce knowledge in fruits of their own' as Coleridge once put it.[1] Immature thinkers they undoubtedly were, yet their thought demanded to be taken seriously. As the year's work progressed, our attention turned more and more frequently to the task of documenting and examining this process of appropriation as it emerged in the activity of the children we were teaching, from day to day and term to term.[2]

It is one particular instance of this study of appropriation, one particular passage of documentation, that I want to use in illustration of the content and style of the research which I have outlined here. My example concerns one of our pupils called Louise and seeks to describe the growth of understanding and of competence that came from her sustained scrutiny of certain aspects of landscape and of landscape painting in the late spring and early summer of 1977, when she was nine and a half years old. The story I have to tell is one among many. In itself it may seem no more than anecdotal. But then, as one of the other contributors to this volume once put it,[3] it may well be one of the major tasks of teacher-based research to 'dignify the anecdote': the moment which gives meaning to reflection and to generalisation. In this respect at least, I believe that anecdote, a richer sense of the particular, is indispensible, both for educational research and for the theory and practice of education as a whole.

The story begins, one morning in early March, when Louise, with her friend Julie, took a walk down to the bottom of the school playing field to make a sketch of one of the tall trees there. The two of them had recently become interested in seeds, shoots, and buds, partly no doubt because of the season and partly because of work which Stephen Rowland had initiated just before half term when he had brought a bag of seeds into the classroom for children to examine and to plant. Their original idea for the walk was to go in search of young plants down the playing field; it was a warm spring day and they wanted to be outside. I had added the idea of sketching a tree when we talked over their plan. I told them to look carefully at the way in which the branches related to the trunk, and to try to draw that.

I was delighted with Louise's sketch, as with Julie's, and

although her subsequent painting was less accurate and delicate than the sketch itself, I felt at the time that it marked a considerable advance on previous paintings of hers. My feeling was confirmed the following week by a second painting which Louise made and which I described as follows in my daily notes.

Monday, March 14th

Louise, at my suggestion, painted a tree again, this time as part of a picture of meadow, flowers, springtime. I wanted to see if the careful sketch she made last week would still reverberate in her painting. It did. She painted enthusiastically, creating a still bolder and more flamboyant tree than last week's (though still without the realism of her sketch), surrounding it with hills, large flowers, and streaks of blue sky. She painted with firm clear strokes of the brush and without preliminary drawing, indicating the sky with streaks of blue, branches with brown flourishes, fields with green blobs and dots. Only the trunk of the tree is filled in with paint; the rest of the picture is all painted outline. This picture has none of the tentativeness that a little while ago seemed so characteristic of Louise. It was painted with speed and panache, though not at all carelessly; up on the classroom wall it stands out easily among the surrounding objects.

This was the first of several paintings of trees in landscapes which Louise made during the spring and summer, and it marked an advance in her thought that was also a new beginning. This first tree has superb presence, dominating the foreground of her painting, the thick upward sweep of its trunk in strong contrast with the loosely swirling branches. It possesses a certain emblematic quality which I had noticed in several children's paintings during that year, a celebration of the object depicted, image of tree. The soft green outlines of hills and the blobs of paint that serve for grassy slopes accentuate the grandeur of the tree at the same time as they lighten the composition as a whole. The elements that make up the picture are relatively simple, even crude, but they are used with considerable verve. Whatever the limitations of her pictorial

Figure 1. Tree

understanding, Louise's painting is in no sense cramped or constrained.

It was in the second week of the summer term, just six weeks after this first large painting of trees in a landscape, that Louise returned to the subject. When I recorded her new painting in my notes I was reminded at once of the earlier picture.

Tuesday, April 26th

I saw nothing of Louise's painting until the end of the day. She had decided to paint first thing in the morning, she and Julie working together again, Julie on a painting of her own, the two of them sitting and painting side by side . . . Louise's picture recalled, in its boldness and charm, her painting of a tree towards the end of last term . . . Unlike the earlier occasion, she had this time begun with a pencilled outline. A little above the centre of a half-sized sheet of green sugar paper she drew a small, square house – central door, four curtained windows, shallow sloping roof, smoking chimney, all strictly according to convention. She set the house on the crest of a line of hills stretching across the paper. On either side of the house, towards the edges of the paper, were large trees, one on the right of the picture on top of the hills and two on the left, one of these low down as if in the foreground, with the other almost directly above it. Despite their different positions within the landscape, all three trees are equally large, with thick tapering trunks and scratched branches inside a rough outline of the overall shape of the treetop. Across the foreground a row of children face stiffly frontways on either side of a picnic hamper and a small rectangle of cloth set with plates and cutlery: peg dolls around a miniature picnic set. The picnic is sketchily drawn, yet is not without a certain detail. Beside the tree on the right are three large flowers – huge, indeed, in relation to the tree. At first I mistook these for standing figures, much to Louise's chagrin.

Louise painted all the trees black. [Two days later she told me this was because there was no brown powder paint ready to hand at the time.] The colour is dense on their trunks, while the treetops are outlined in black and filled in with a few thin black strokes. The bold, black forms dominate the picture on either side. The hills between are painted in blobs of green, as in her earlier picture, but this time their distant outlines are pencilled rather than painted. As for the house on the hill, only its roof is painted, pale mauve, while the picnickers and their picnic are not painted at all. The three huge flowers are orange, green and black. At the top of the picture Louise has added, as before, cloudlike smudges of blue paint, representing a deep blue sky. The painting has amplified the drawn picture, enhancing its feeling of distance and space. Looking at it now, on the floor beside me as I write, I find in it a haunting, almost lonely quality, despite the picnic: a sense of remoteness. This effect is perhaps partly accidental, a consequence of the colours chosen for want of others readily available, the areas unpainted because, as Louise explained to

Figure 2. Landscape with picnic

me, of the difficulty of painting them, the very crudity of the brush strokes themselves. But the accident is organised; it reflects the intended as well as the unintended effects of Louise's particular decisions; it is a product, I think, of the thoughtfulness with which she has painted.

Two days later Louise wrote a few brief lines of description to accompany her picture. It is interesting to observe how in her writing she takes up the very aspect of the picture that, in its painted form, had seemed least significant: its narrative element. Thus, it was the picnic that she chose to describe rather than the landscape itself. It was only later, at my suggestion, that she added two lines about the house on the hill and the flanking trees:

> people eating their picnic on the sunny grass
> boys and girls climbing trees
> boys and girls running around the trees
> flowers growing, people picking them
> the house far away in the distance
> trees blowing side by side.

It is as if in her painting the narrative is a background to the landscape while in her writing the painted landscape has itself become a background for narrative. The simple phrases and images capture the mood of a summer picnic very well. They would have been an appropriate expression of the class's own summer picnic later that term in a large wood a few miles from the school. Narrative and landscape were to be brought together in similar ways in two further paintings by Louise, as we shall see.

Although it reminded me of her earlier painting of a tree in a landscape, there are several points of difference between this painting and the previous one. For example, the landscape has been brought into the forefront of the picture and is a more pervasive presence. It is no longer merely the decorative background for a portrait of a tree, but the setting for a picnic, and it is the setting rather than the picnic that dominates the picture. The trees are still the most dramatic element in the painted landscape but they have been pushed towards the sides of the painting and placed within the landscape rather than in front of it – though still without regard to perspective. Moreover, their predominance is counterbalanced to some extent by the house on the hill between them, which asserts itself by virtue of its central position within the composition, in spite of the fact that only its roof is painted. (Indeed, the decision to paint the roof alone seems to me, if anything, to draw further attention to the distant house.) The combination of drawing and painting is a further point of difference between this painting and the last, as is the introduction of an element of narrative, however muted. But the chief difference lies in the compositional balance of the two paintings. Both display a strong sense of form, but in the second the forms are disposed in a more complex and more subtle way.

Each of these differences was to be sharpened further in Louise's fourth painting of trees in a landscape, which seemed to begin where this second picture left off and to represent a more powerful variation on the same compositional themes. In the meantime, however, just a week after her second picture, she had painted trees yet again, this time in a manner more severe

Figure 3. Tree, grass, river, sky

than anything she had yet attempted. I know nothing about the origin of this third painting or about the way in which it was painted. I noticed it at the end of the day on which it was painted but I did not see Louise painting it and I never discussed it with her. Two days previously we had paid one of several visits to a nearby river bank and I think that the blue strip in the painting probably represents a river, so that the picture may have stemmed from Louise's experience on that day, though I cannot be sure. Nor do I know for sure whether the pink smudges of paint between and across the branches of the two trees represent a sunset sky, although I suspect that they do.

There was no preliminary drawing on this occasion. Two black trees fill the paper, side by side, with wedge-shaped trunks and scrawny branches recalling her first tree painting. They rest on a strip of grass which was once again painted by a series of blobs and splotches, using the top of the paintbrush. The grass is painted over the black base of the trees and an inch or two up their sides, conveying a certain impression of depth. A little further up the picture there is a thick blue strip which runs across the page, interrupted by the trees: a river, as I suppose, passing behind the trunks. The only other features are three bright pink smudges, perhaps a sunset sky, which cross the branches towards the top of the painting.

Trees, grass, river, sky: landscape has here been reduced to a few elementary particulars represented by the barest means. The painting has the appearance of a sketch, and it might be tempting to pass it off, for all its starkness, as unfinished or less considered in comparison with its two predecessors, if it were not for the fact that it represents a style to which Louise was to return right at the end of term, one of two contrasting styles in which she chose to represent trees in a landscape. In her next painting, however, she returned to the style and treatment of her earlier landscape. As before, her new painting was associated with a fragment of writing, but on this occasion it was the writing that led to the painting rather than the reverse.

The writing described 'a tree on a windy day':

> On a windy day the wind blows in and out of the trees, the
> leaves fall down and go into the grass, the branches snap,
> the workman saws the trees down.

It is a precise evocation, encompassing not only the windy day but its consequences – the trees which, their branches snapped, have to be sawn down. I was struck by the clarity of Louise's vocabulary: the branches 'snap', the wind blows 'in and out of' the trees, the falling leaves go 'into' the grass. The same clarity and precision can be observed in the large painting which illustrated and elaborated Louise's writing.

Tuesday, May 17th

Louise followed the writing with a large accompanying painting, the latest in what is now a formidable sequence of tree pictures. The painting recalls her last but one picture: the picnic between three trees, amid grassy hills with the prospect of a distant house. As in each of her two previous paintings, the trees are black, the colour she originally chose for want of

Figure 4. Trees on a windy day

brown but now seems to be choosing for its own sake. (I remember how, when Louise told me that she had painted the three trees in her picnic landscape black because there was no brown paint to be had, Karen, who was sitting next to her as we talked, butted in that she liked their blackness anyway.) Hills and houses are there again also, but this time the grassy hills are depicted by a single thick green outline and there are no fewer than three houses atop them, the smoke from their chimneys blowing strongly rightwards, while the two central trees in the foreground of the picture bend to the left. In a somewhat pedantic schoolteacher's way I pointed out the discrepancy to Louise who at once saw it as a 'mistake'. But on reflection it was I who was mistaken. The contrast in the direction of smoke and trees enhances the formal rhythm of the painting, nor incidentally is there any reason why, on a blustery day, distant smoke and nearby branches should necessarily be blowing in the same direction.

In the foreground, at the bottom of the large sheet of brown sugar paper, stand four black trees, evenly distributed in a row across the painting. The two outermost trees are straight, one on either side of the paper, their tops outlined like poplars, the branches indicated by scattered brush strokes inside the lozenge-shaped outlines, after the manner of the trees in the landscape with picnic. By contrast, the two inner trees have long thick branches which bend before the wind, and their tops are not outlined. They resemble the two trees in Louise's last painting rather than those in the picnic landscape. The trunk of the straight tree on the right is surrounded by short brush strokes – Stephen watched Louise applying them with great care – representing, as Louise explained to me, the branches that had snapped, as her writing puts it, rather than the falling leaves for which I had mistaken them. Between and above the two inner trees a few scattered leaves are blowing about. At one point I suggested to Louise that she might add more, as the middle of the painting seemed to me (at the time, though no longer) a little sparse, or 'empty'; this was how Louise had described to me the unfilled space in her last painting. She did add more leaves, but very few. At the foot of the trees, across the bottom of the picture, she has painted tall blades of grass 'into' which, as in her description, one or two leaves are already falling. The tree at the left of the painting is being sawn down by two workmen, rudimentary figures as in the picnic landscape and, as before, unpainted. When I asked Louise about these she said that she didn't really want to paint them, I suspect because she would have found this difficult or because she was conscious of the discrepancy between these figures and the rest of the forms in the painting. On the crest of the two outlined hills the three houses have black windows, doors, chimney pots, and smoke, while their roofs and walls are outlined in pencil only. Above them float the deep blue smudges of sky familiar from Louise's previous paintings, four of them this time.

This picture of trees on a windy day marks the climax of Louise's sequence of landscapes with trees. There is a richness of treatment in the painting which seems to embody all of her previous explorations of this theme in the preceding weeks. Many of the painting's individual motifs are the same as in the landscape with picnic: the softly curving hills, distant houses, black trees, unpainted scarecrow figures suggestive of narrative, the association of picture and written word. But these several motifs are here rearranged into a more dramatic and elaborated whole, almost as if the previous painting were being used as a preparatory study. In discussing the earlier picture, for example, I drew attention to the element of accident in the painting itself, in such details as the absence of brown paint, the painting of only the roof of the house, the ignoring of the pencilled figures, and I suggested that part of Louise's achievement lay in her ability to turn such accidents to good effect. But the accidents or half-accidents of the landscape with picnic have become deliberate effects in the landscape of trees on a windy day. The colour black is now chosen for its own sake, for the starkness of its quality. It is not only the trees that are black but the leaves, the snapping branches, the houses and smoke. (One leaf, it can be seen, was originally painted green. Louise has carefully painted out the green, on second thoughts.) Once again the hilltop houses are only partly painted but this time Louise has selected what to paint with deliberate care: the apertures and appendages of the buildings – doors, windows, chimney pots. There is, altogether, a notable economy about Louise's choice of what to paint in her picture: the bare contour of the hills, a detail which had remained no more than a faint, blurred pencil line in the picnic landscape; the blown smoke; the tall blades of grass into which the leaves can be seen falling in correspondence with the written lines accompanying the picture; the straight, snapped sticks; and the few curly leaves carefully scattered across the picture surface. Her treatment of the trees which once more dominate her landscape is particularly interesting. The familiar wedge-shaped trunks have disappeared while the two distinct types of treetop developed in the previous three landscapes are here brought together within the same painting for the first time, to great effect.

In this, her fourth successive landscape, Louise has extended her pictorial range by fusing into one the contrasting styles of

her last two paintings, the stark calligraphy of the landscape
with two trees by a river and the broader treatment of her
landscape with picnic, with its more scenic conception and its
touch of narrative. In its specifically human aspect the narrative
is still muted, the two workmen being left unpainted, almost as
if Louise found it awkward to accommodate human figures
within such an elemental picture; but in other respects the
correspondence between word and image is more exact and
more detailed, possibly in part because the painting came after
the writing rather than before. Nowhere is Louise's growing
assurance more evident than in the formal organisation of the
landscape. The increasing subtlety already noticeable in the
landscape with picnic is taken a stage further. Consider the way
in which the two straight outer trees frame the windswept
branches of the two inner trees; the counterpoint between the
leftward-bending branches and the rightward-blowing smoke;
the contrast between the long green curve of the hills and the
thicket of straight green grasses below the trees. These formal
contrasts embody the drama of the landscape no less than do the
individual details which make up its subject matter, or the
correspondences between image and word.

There followed now a pause in Louise's landscape painting, as
if she had for the moment exhausted her chosen theme, having
worked out her ideas in painting after painting with increasing
understanding. In the weeks that followed she turned her
attention to new subjects and techniques: a large, unfinished
painting of a church; bark rubbings; a collage picture of a house,
at which she worked with another girl in the class; a cardboard
model room with model furniture. Twice before the end of term
however she returned to the theme of landscape, in drawings
and paintings which reflected the assurance and control that she
had derived from the practice of landscape painting over the
previous three months. The first episode was on June 9th, the
day after half term, when a group of twelve children, Louise
among them, went down to the nearby river again to work.
Louise had chosen to make sketches of the river bank and had
taken with her pencil, paper, and a piece of hardboard to which
she secured her paper by means of an elastic band. She began by

Figure 5. Tree sketch

drawing one of the trees on the bank; I can still recall the way she stood, a little in front of the tree, staring intently at it as she drew. Later that afternoon she made a second sketch, of the river winding away beyond the bridge. She stood on the bridge to draw this time, her hardboard propped against the parapet.

In my note about that afternoon's work I described her two drawings as 'further evidence of her increasing power of visual representation'. In sketching the tree Louise ignored its leaves and concentrated all her attention on the disposition of its branches. Some branches are carefully detailed; others are cut short once their line has been established; still others fan out into

Figure 6. River sketch

thickets of rough lines. The angle at which the two main branches break away from the trunk is drawn with particular precision. Trunk and branches are shaded in with the pencil and in places Louise seems to have attempted to indicate rough hollows, scratches or protuberances on the bark. I noticed at the time how advanced the drawing was in naturalness by comparison with her first tree sketch the previous term.

The second sketch, of the winding river, is looser in treatment. It has an improvisatory quality, as if it were drawn with a certain abandon. The drawing is a mass of scribbles and squiggles, some heavy, others rather faint; rough pencil marks out of which emerges an image of river and bank. The bend in the river is portrayed with great confidence, as also is the motley collection of trees, bushes, reeds, and lily pads at the water's edge.

When we returned to the classroom Louise put the drawings away in her tray and it was not until a fortnight later that she noticed them again:

Figure 7. River (painted version)

Thursday, June 23rd

First thing this morning Louise had been wanting an idea as to how to begin her day's work. In her drawer she found the two drawings she had made down at the river the day after half term. She brought them to me and asked what she should do with them. I told her to put them in her folder and then asked if she would like to turn the sketch of the river curving away from the bridge into a painting, something both she and I had had in mind after the river trip but which she had never got round to doing. She was keen, so we collected a sheet of sugar paper – she chose green – and she began. First she drew an enlarged sketch onto the paper. The way she copied her original sketch was different from the way she had turned her last term's tree sketch into a painting. Then, the relationship between sketch and painting had been a little distant, the painting less precise and less naturalistic. Now, whether because of the gap in time between sketch and painting, or the nature of the sketch, or the growth of her skill in the meantime, she copied the drawing almost exactly, enlarged, onto the sugar paper. The curving river was the same, with the same banks, trees, bushes, reeds, lily pads, and the same four-barred gate in the top right-hand corner. Her only change, a significant one, was to add several figures to the meadow beside the river – matchstick figures as all her figures still are.

Then she began to paint, starting with the river and its lily pads, the lily pads first, carefully filled in in green, and then the river around them. (Later, perhaps because she was dissatisfied with the roughness of the blue paint around the lily pads, she painted over the lily pads, repainting them once she had finished the river itself.) For the river she mixed her own shade of blue. When the river was painted she added black ripples, black stumps of reeds, and, to the right of the river, three new green lily pads. Next she painted the bushes and trees, dabbing the paint on rather than filling in the outlines. Finally she tackled the meadow on the left of the river and the rougher banks on the right, using splodges of green for the meadow and of dark brown for the banks on the other side. The left-hand bank, below the meadow, was a thick brown fringe. I watched her as she painted meadow and banks. She applied the paint freely, with no doubt as to what effect she wanted or how to achieve it. Then she stood back looking at her painting and I asked her if it was finished. It was, she said. I pointed to the unpainted figures. They weren't to be painted, she said. I pointed to an unpainted tree on the bank. Yes, she'd paint that, she said, and she did, although afterwards I felt that perhaps she had been right, whether by accident or design, to leave it unpainted originally. [At this time I paid little attention to the various unpainted figures which Louise had added to the picture. It was only later that their significance struck me. They were the characters who had peopled that landscape on the afternoon on which she drew her sketch: a pram, which Stephen Rowland's wife, who

Figure 8. Tree (painted version)

had come with us, had brought for her baby; a girl holding what could be a notebook but is almost certainly intended to be the hardboard with an elastic band across it which Louise had with her; two children with fishing nets used for collecting water insects; and a small stray figure perhaps intended to be Stephen's two-year-old son. In turning the sketch into a full-blown painting Louise had thus changed it from a simple landscape of the winding river into the story of the afternoon's activity. As with earlier landscapes the narrative is muted, both because of the decision to leave the figures unpainted and because of the matchstick quality of the figures themselves, so different from the naturalism of the landscape in which they are placed. Nevertheless, the narrative intention is plain and was certainly deliberate.]

Both in the way she painted and in the quality of the

finished painting Louise shows, I think, how far she has grown intellectually during the year. When I pinned the picture up on the wall she asked for the drawing to be pinned up alongside it. Then, after morning play, she decided to paint a version of her second sketch, that of the tree. Once again she copied the sketch closely, painting the tree brown now rather than black and leaving it, as in the sketch, leafless and with several of its branches cut short, as if broken off. Above it, she added three streaks of blue sky and, in the top left-hand corner, a simple round yellow sun, without the face, rays, hat, or pipe, so commonplace, still, with the class. And that was all. Yes, that was all she wanted, she told me. The painting is austere, most of the green sugar paper unpainted and the colours simple and thick. There are no added adornments except for the round disc of the sun, no attempt at narrative as in the painting of the river. This picture, too, we pinned up with the sketch alongside it. It will probably mark the conclusion of Louise's thoughts about painting and about landscape for the year.

And so, indeed, it did.

REFERENCES

Note: A version of the second part of this chapter appeared in the American journal Outlook, no 36, Summer 1980.
1. The Friend, ed. Barbara E. Rooke, Routledge and Kegan Paul, 1969, Vol I, p. 473
2. For a full account of this enquiry see Closely Observed Children, Michael Armstrong, Writers and Readers, 1981
3. Raymond Verrier, speaking at a conference on The Role of the Teacher in Research, held at Fircroft College, Birmingham, 16–19 November 1979

LEE ENRIGHT

The diary of a classroom

Any teacher embarking upon an action research project faces the problem of when, how and what to record: before, during or after the lesson; emotions, facts, dilemmas or surprises. This problem was particularly acute in my case because my research was a response to general, but nevertheless urgent, concerns. These centred on the way in which children use ideas to solve problems for themselves, how these ideas might be shared through more effective group discussion, and how the teacher might collaborate with the pupils in the learning that goes on in the classroom.

Since, at the outset of the research, I was not at all sure what data would help me explore these questions, I decided to record as much detail as I could about everything that happened in my class. During the first half of the summer term of 1978 I began to keep a diary. I wrote this up daily, a task which required between two and three hours every evening. Maggie Gracie, who was the deputy head of the school, also taught my class and was able to take an active part in the research. She read through my entries regularly and added her own comments where she felt necessary. Her moral and professional support proved invaluable.

The following year I repeated the diary. I had moved with my class up into the third year and it seemed an opportunity not to be missed to repeat the exercise with the same group of children a year later. Moreover, several questions remained from the previous summer. In particular I had become very interested in the part played by talk and discussion in learning and I wanted to examine what happened in my class. Because it still took two to three hours each night the diary was again restricted to the first seven weeks of the summer term. Nevertheless, in that short time I still managed to fill five A4 files.

It is now two years since I wrote the first diary and one year since I wrote the second. Reading through them produces a variety of sensations; some of the events I can hardly remember, while others are recalled in detail by a single sentence. The person writing the diaries could almost be someone else; someone who was obviously very excited by what was happening and who had the good fortune to work in an atmosphere of support and encouragement. All the data given here comes straight from my diaries; some are quoted directly, others are paraphrases.

West Moors Middle School (9–13), where I still teach, opened in September 1977. The second year group with which I worked contained 83 children in three mixed ability groups. During both the second and third years part of the integrated studies programme consists of the social studies curriculum known as 'Man: A Course of Study'. This course was developed by the educationist, Jerome Bruner, and sets out to explore three questions: What is Man? How did he get that way? How can he be made more so? The course materials are drawn from contemporary studies of animal and human behaviour, and provide examples of contrast and comparison to help children develop their own ideas on the three key questions. My class followed the Salmon and Herring Gull units of the course during the second year and the Baboon and Netsilik Eskimo units in their third year.

By using extracts from the two diaries I shall try to illuminate certain key issues which, in retrospect, seem to have preoccupied me throughout the period I taught this particular class. Clearly, these issues are interwoven and cannot be treated in isolation. Frequently each crops up in the discussion of a single classroom event. The following extract, for example, raises a number of issues by highlighting the pupils' ability to initiate ideas for themselves through discussion with the teacher.

Stuart, Martin P, Mark M, Christopher, Brian and Russell wanted to make an environment board of the tundra. I asked if one of them would keep a note of their plans, and Stuart said he would. I returned to the boys some time after, when Stuart was having to work pretty hard to keep up with the group. He asked if he ought to tape the discussion as that would make his job easier – he'd never remember otherwise. I almost agreed, but then asked if it would be easier if I sat in on the discussion and took notes. They said they thought it probably would.

Martin P said that they had all agreed that the base ought to be heavy card.

Stuart said the surface should be papier-mâché, and the rest agreed.

At this point I suggested that it might be a good idea to have a look at one of the Netsilik unit films to remind ourselves what the tundra looked like. They said yes, and Stuart and Russell went off to get the projector and the film cartridge of 'Fishing at the Stone Weir'.

Mark M said that lakes would have to be included on the board.

Martin P got quite excited at the idea of lining part of the board with polythene so that 'real' water could be used.

Brian remembered an experiment we did in the Science Area, heating up ammonium dichromate which then fountained out tiny greeny-brown granules, but this idea was discounted as being 'no good'. I comforted Brian with the fact that although the stuff was the right colour, we wouldn't be able to use it because it was too expensive.

Christopher said he had some pebbles to bring in for the Stone Weir.

He then said we could use real grass, but I thought it would probably die.

Martin P said we needed to make some leather tents.

Mark M said he had some pieces of leather at home that he can bring in.

Stuart wondered if we would have a backdrop which would show the sky.

(By now the film was set up and we were watching it. A bird had just flown across a brilliant blue sky.)

Christopher said we could use dead grass and chop it.

Brian noticed some large rocks in the distance, and said we would have to include those.

Stuart then considered how to make the Stone Weir. He thought the best way would be to make most of it out of plasticene, and then have a couple of layers of stones showing above the water.

Martin P said he felt we ought to have a couple of men in the river.

Stuart suggested we make them out of pipe-cleaners.

Martin P told him we wanted to use 'real' water (Stuart had been out getting the film when this was mentioned) so pipe cleaners would be no good. He thought that plastic covered wire would be better.

I expressed some doubt. Then—

Brian said he had some Play-people at home that he could bring in.

There was some amazement that Brian still plays with Play-people – Martin P said that his little brother plays with them.

Brian said so what? He (Brian) plays with Lego too.

Martin P said that Play-people are all *men* (can this be true?) so we would have to make a wig for the woman.

I mentioned how cold the water was as we watched the men in the river.

Brian said we had better make sure that the water on the environment board was 'real cold' too. He added (to me) that Play-people are all the same size – there wasn't one we could use for the fisherman's little boy.

Stuart suggested that we push him down into the papier-mâché, so that he is only half the size of the adults. Laughter!

Martin P said that the levels of water were different on either side of the stone weir. We would have to slope the papier-mâché base accordingly.

Brian said we could turn over the environment board we had made during our work on Baboons.

Stuart said that we should use tinfoil on the base under the water, as this would reflect the way water does.

When I read through all that the boys talked about that session, I was astonished by their ability to include so many aspects of building an environment board of the tundra. Their discussion included decisions about co-operation, artistic effect, geographical accuracy, and also showed how they were able to consider the people who live in the tundra.

When I joined the group I was informed that they had all agreed that the base should be heavy card and the surface papier-mâché. So often it is this first decision that is removed from children 'to get them going', yet it *can* act as a unifying factor when the group makes that decision itself, and thus give the group an extra boost forward. As the boys made their various suggestions about what materials could be used on the board, there was very little rejection. This only happened when I vetoed using ammonium dichromate, and when I seemed doubtful about using plastic covered wire. Generally, suggestions were accepted with more or less enthusiasm; when Christopher's idea about grass seemed problematic he didn't get annoyed or upset, but carried on thinking about it, and then offered an adapted version which was accepted.

The boys also showed great care about making the board look good. They wanted to use papier-mâché because they said it would be 'better'. As the work continued over the next few weeks, in spite of the difficulties they had about getting the papier-mâché dried out properly, they frequently remarked that papier-mâché helped you get the ground to look the way it should. Martin P wanted to use 'real' water – he felt that paint just wouldn't be right. He also wanted the tents made in leather – because that's how they are. Plastic Play-people were considered as the fisherman and his family, and while Stuart's suggestion that one of them should be pushed down to half its size caused a good deal of laughter, the sense of the idea was obvious. Martin P also wanted it to be quite clear which one of the Play-people was the woman – not usually the main consideration of a group of eleven year old boys. Stuart was keen that the water should be as realistic as possible, and put forward the idea that tin foil would be best to represent the reflective ability of water.

The boys' discussion also showed how they grasped the main ideas about the geographical features of the tundra. They were aware of the different size rocks that are found on the tundra. Martin P saw that the water levels were different on either side of the stone weir. They knew what colour and texture was necessary for the ground. No one suggested including trees.

On another occasion, three boys – Mark W, Martin O and Roy – had great success through ignoring the conventional restrictions involved in monoprinting. On the first occasion, Mark W and Roy asked if they could use two colours instead of the standard one colour – hence monoprint. I said I did not think it would work unless they could really mask off one area from the other. Some time later they showed me a beautiful duoprint for which they had used blue and brown.

The next day Roy had really caught the bug with this work. His first print used three colours, but was not as successful as his duoprint – probably because he did not press hard enough. However, he carried on, saying that how he would do one with four colours.

Roy prepared what he called his 'Shepherd's Sunset': Martin O was allowed to help achieve the artistic effect. The sky was blue first, then some white was added with a finger and mixed slightly. Red was added in spots, and then all the colours were mixed until Roy was happy. We got two prints off the board, both of which are very pleasing.

This episode made me realise that however 'crazy' or impracticable children's ideas may appear, they often produce work which is of very high quality. This incident encouraged me to be more accepting of apparently inapplicable ideas, and thus encouraged the children to come up with them. Children in my subsequent classes have benefited from this approach, and I have also found it works with other members of staff in my teaching team.

Knowing when and how to intervene often poses problems when teachers are trying to encourage children towards finding their own solutions. Maggie and I came to the conclusion that when the problem is one that the teacher has no immediate answer to, it is perfectly reasonable to join in with the children's speculation.

It should be made quite clear to children, though, that your speculations are just that – they are not directives. It is also true that if children know that they are free to ignore your suggestions, the intervention becomes less crucial.

Tracy, Sarah T and Theresa asked if they could use a flower press. I said there wasn't one belonging to the school. I thought Fiona owned one, but it turned out that she had left it at home. Did they fancy making one? They did! Unfortunately, we had no butterfly nuts in school either, but they improvised a way of putting pressure on their flower samples.

They put them between thick sheets of corrugated card and jumped up and down on them! This certainly flattened the flowers, but a) it didn't dry them sufficiently, and b) jumping up and down with both feet landing on the same spot repeatedly is, in Sarah T's words, 'Knackering!'

At this point, I remembered Maggie's brick collection. She has been collecting examples of unusual or 'limited edition' house bricks, and these are kept in her office. I sent the girls to ask if they could borrow some bricks.

Theresa, Tracy and Sarah T collected their flowers from Maggie's office today. Because of the week's half-term holiday, the flowers were pressed for nearly a fortnight. The girls were very pleased with the result. They said they weren't going to put them in their books. They wanted to mount them on something. While they were still sorting them out, I noticed the store of polystyrene in the corner of the Art Area, which adjoins the Science Laboratory where we were working.

I went over to look for a decent sized piece, and found one which had two circles and two rectangles cut out of it. I took it in and suggested they arrange some sugar paper in the spaces (the rectangles and circles were all in rectangular recesses), but Sarah T said they could put the sugar paper at the back of the holes so that it would show through – brilliant! I left them to it.

Once you begin to accept that children are adept at solving their difficulties, it is easy to become over-excited and start concentrating on your own feelings. This never occurred to me until I started to look at myself as a teacher by keeping the diary. For instance, on one occasion some boys in my class faced the problem of how to make arrows go further. I became too excited to think about the effect I was having on their discussion, which was tape-recorded and then transcribed for inclusion in my diary. However, as soon as I listened to the tape, I began to realise what I had done. Russell had made thirteen contributions, Stuart had made seven, Mark K three, and I had made twenty-four – more than all three boys put together. I had also interrupted six times. I had not realised just how easy it is to dominate children's conversation and discussion. Now I find that I can learn about children's ideas by listening and by using eye contact to bring in other members of the group. Before I heard this tape and transcribed it, I hadn't understood that being excited and positive about what is being discussed can be just as damaging as holding 'discussions' held along the 'leading questions' lines.

Just before I began keeping the first diary, Maggie and I decided that we had to do something to improve the quality of discussion in my class. Maggie noted that she 'found it difficult to get any kind of order into a discussion. Children wanted to contribute at the same time, and did not seem to listen to each other's contributions'. Like many other teachers, I had tried discussion lessons – and abandoned them as complete failures.

We decided that the best way for us to help the children towards an orderly discussion was to tape it. Each child had to wait for the microphone to be aimed at him before he was able to speak. When we transcribed this tape, we were able to see where things were going wrong. Children were aiming their contributions at *us*, taking little notice of each other.

Putting the children into small groups for discussion seemed to be the answer – but how should these small groups be made up? Mixed-ability, mixed-sex groups? Single-sex friendship groups? Permanent or temporary groupings? During the time I kept the diaries, I began to find the information which has helped me towards much greater success in discussion work.

While the children were in the Second Year, they worked on the 'Structure and Function' section in 'Man: A Course of Study'. In this section they are asked to examine unfamiliar objects, consider their structure and speculate about their possible functions. The children worked in small groups for this work. I spent some of one lesson working with Brian and his friends. I noted in the diary: 'Brian found it difficult to pay attention to the object *except when he was actually handling it*, so I kept moving it on from one to the other.'

At about the same time in the Second Year, Mark C became very interested in tape-recording stories instead of writing them. The stories were exciting, and very fluently told without resorting to the pause button on the tape recorder. Maggie wrote in the diary:

> I passed through the Hall while he was playing the tape back to himself, and I stopped to listen. I made some vague comments and then asked him if he had taped it straight off. 'Yes.' Had he had the story in his head? 'No.' I admired the sound effects he had added to his story. He produced a little man on a keyring, and explained and demonstrated how the little person had been animated while he made the noises. Did the little person help him make the experience concrete?

These two incidents helped me realise that children need to be surrounded by concrete aids to learning – the object Brian was speculating about *had* to be in his hands; to tell a story you need an audience – some children need that audience to be immediate – like Mark's little man. Maggie's active participation in the research meant that this second incident was discussed and recorded in detail along with the rest of the day's events.

When I moved up with the children into the Third Year, I felt that whole class discussion *could* work, and tried to make it do so, but I didn't abandon small group work. Sometimes, however, the nature of the work meant that the children had to work in small groups, and on one of these occasions I used tape recorders to record all seven working groups.

They were working on the Netsilik eskimo unit, and their task was to design a vehicle that would travel over snow and ice. They *had to* use fish, thong, caribou antlers, caribou bones, moss and hide, all of which were illustrated on small cards given to each group. The groups had to draw their vehicle on to an overhead projector transparency, and one member had to pre-sent the design to the rest of the class after about twenty minutes.

That lesson contained groupings which were single-sex friendship groups, mixed sex and ability non-friendship groups, and mixed sex and ability friendship groups. Some of the groups were working together for the first time, and some of them had worked together regularly. The tape transcripts astonished me. All the groups understood the task, answered it, and were able to report back to the rest of the class at the right time. In only one group did a child let the presence of the tape recorder distract him (in spite of the fact that he used a tape recorder regularly in his language work) and so disturb the group. His group's tape showed that their discussion had not been as intense as many of the other groups, and that it was frequently interrupted by this boy – but the task seemed to draw them back each time.

My conclusions, as a result of the research I did at this time, are that groupings appear to be one of the least important factors for good discussion. I think the most important factors are that the children understand the task, that they see its relevance, that they understand how they will have to report back, and that – if possible – they have something *real* to help focus their attention. Something 'real' need not be physically present; it can be the children's own experience that we ask them to bring to the discussion, but it can also be as real as Mark's keyring or the picture cards used in the sledge-building exercise.

The next extract describes events which took place while the children were examining the plants and animals that could be found in our school grounds. *What* they studied was less important to us than *the way* they studied it. We wanted them to record their own observations and speculations, and not just rely on secondary source material. These lessons were led by our science specialist, Clive Thompson.

I went back into the Science Area, almost getting knocked over by Sarah T in yet another high state of excitement. She was carrying a jar of water out to somewhere in the school grounds, why I don't know. I didn't stop her to ask because I was just as excited – about something *I* had decided to do.

I wanted to make a maze or choice chamber for woodlice. I think it will work. Strips of thin card are used for the walls, supported by pins stuck into a thick block of polystyrene. I got a vast chunk of polystyrene from the Art Area, cut my strips of card, collected some dressmaker's pins [the Science, Art and Home Education Areas all interconnect] and went back to the Science Area to make a start.

Stuart and Christopher had also started to make a maze, but weren't too happy with the way it was going. They talked of abandoning it, but I said that having hacked into a goodish cardboard box, they ought not to give up so easily. They are both amiable boys, and they set about the task again without rancour. Christopher was watching me pretty carefully as I was setting up the walls of my maze. He said he liked the idea(!) and talked to Stuart about trying it out on their maze. I agreed to share my pins.

All too soon came the end of the morning, and the class had to be prised away from the work. So did the teacher.

[Next session:] As I began work on my maze today, I noticed that Stuart and Christopher had brought theirs with them but were not working on it. In his Science book last week, Christopher had written that the maze had not succeeded. I had written underneath, 'How could you change it to make it succeed?' I asked him if he had read my comment. He had. Well? Stuart protested that the card did not stay on the floor of the maze, so the ant just crawled underneath the walls. 'How could you stop that?' I asked. 'Plasticene?' he answered.

Leaving them to decide exactly how they would use the plasticene, I went off to collect the pins I needed and some plasticene for them. When I looked some time later, they were rolling sausages of plasticene, arranging them in the cardboard box, and then sticking the strips of card into these sausages.

I returned to work on my maze. Mark C, Mark W and Bryan were looking at the woodlice they gathered last week, and arguing about what they ought to be doing while I finished my maze. First of all, as they obviously wanted to do *something*, I suggested they go and find a couple more woodlice – Mark W also insisted they needed some more twigs. When they returned I was almost finished, so I asked them to think of something they could find out about by putting a woodlouse into the maze.

Bryan said he wanted to see if the woodlouse would follow a trail of sugar.

Mark C said he wanted to see if a woodlouse would try to hide under stones or pieces of wood which were put into the maze.

Mark W wanted to look at the paths the woodlouse took through the maze. Would it, for instance, go back on itself a lot?

Bryan was making a note of these ideas and, having written down Mark W's, said, 'Miss Enright?' I looked up, not sure what he meant. 'What experiment are *you* going to do?' I was hoist by my own petard – I had been so intent on the sheer joy of making the maze that I hadn't even bothered to think what *I* would use it for! The three boys saw my uncertainty and laughed – as I did!

I decided that I would look at the effect on the woodlouse of a beam of light from a torch. Would I be able to make it avoid certain channels by shining a bright light on them?

We tried Mark C's experiment. At first, the woodlouse stopped for about half a minute under a piece of wood, but then it moved on again. Sometimes it crawled under stones, sometimes it crawled over them. Once, to Mark W's surprise, it walked backwards. Mark W didn't think that an animal with so many legs would be able to do this. He also noticed that the woodlouse slipped off a stone – 'It can't grip things,' he said.

We tried out Mark W's experiment. We found that the woodlouse stayed in more or less the same channels. Several times it returned to the edge of the maze at the point where it had been put in at the beginning of the experiment. Mark W had had a vague hope that it would find its way to the other side of the maze, and said that his experiment had failed. I tried to explain that you *couldn't* fail when you were simply watching like this, but he didn't seem convinced.

We tried out my experiment. At first the woodlouse did, once, move away from the light, but this turned out to be sheer coincidence because it never recurred. Clive suggested that the woodlouse was already in what amounted to intense light. I suggested we try the experiment in the Drama Studio under complete blackout. Unfortunately, there was a drama lesson going on, so I settled for the curtained P.E. equipment store in the Hall. Again, the woodlouse ignored the light. Mark C said it was because this woodlouse was probably the oldest (i.e. we had had it longest) and so it wouldn't take any notice of the light. Bryan suggested that they store the woodlouse in the dark for a while and then try the experiment again. The other two boys agreed, and Bryan put the wood-lice on the top shelf in my cupboard, assuring me that they would be quite safe there, because they didn't try to escape before, did they?

Bryan's experiment wasn't tried because we ran out of time.

Participating as a learner in Clive's lessons gave me a real insight into what goes on in a class. As teachers we are often trying to inspire children with the joy of learning, but how often do we let them see *us* experiencing that joy? The teacher as a model of a learner has great potential – it keeps the teacher aware of how it feels to be a learner; it helps the children move away from the idea that the teacher has all the answers; it helps to prove that the world is so exciting that even people as old as teachers can discover new things.

Working as a pupil while another teacher takes the lead demands that the class teacher 'let go' and trust that other teacher to look after the children. Initially, I found this one of the hardest things to do. Surely no one else knew who the potential skivers were? Who needed help with spelling? Who needed to be persuaded against seven visits to the toilets every hour? By the time I came to work with Clive in the Science Area, I had had sufficient experience of this to realise that I was surrounded by teachers who were just as competent as I believed myself to be. I had also learnt to allow myself to become excited by the *prospect* of taking part.

Noise is often thought to be a problem when a teacher has a class working in small discussion groups. The worry is not just about disturbing surrounding classes, but whether children can actually concentrate in all that racket. At one point when I was working in Maggie's lesson on the Bushman language, I realised I was surrounded by an amount of noise that could be considered as less than acceptable. Within seconds, I was back to the task we had been set. I knew what I was doing, I was enjoying doing it, and other people's noise had no effect on our group's work.

While I was working on the maze in the Science lesson, it became clear that the most important thing to me was *making* the maze. The process of solving the problems of building something that woodlice couldn't crawl under or through was a real delight. During those two sessions in the Science Area I think I learnt something about the relationship between pins, card, polystyrene and woodlice, and although I was quite interested in using the maze in my light beam experiment, it is the building process that stands out in my mind. The work we had planned for the children was about observing mini-beasts and plants – not about building things to observe them in. I was lucky enough to be in an environment that considered my interest in building a maze to be as important as the work that was programmed.

The excitement I experienced as a participant helped me realise the importance of *planning* teacher participation in children's work, particularly when the experience is likely to be a new one for the teacher. Teachers are often unsure about their role in such sessions, but it is marvellous to see them getting excited with the work, to see them looking to the children when they get stuck, and to hear them afterwards describing how they managed to overcome insurmountable problems! Participation could also help teachers who can't resist 'helping' children – particularly in art and craft work. If you've got your own model to make, your itchy fingers stay away from the children's work, and it's easier to help the children find their own solutions.

I wrote the diaries while working full time in the classroom. I would argue that it is not necessary for a teacher to withdraw from teaching before carrying out useful research. Much that is valuable can only be carried out by the teacher who is working in the class. Keeping the diaries forced me to look more closely at myself, the children and our interaction. It has made me think twice about the things I say and do in the classroom. Further, the research enhanced my understanding of problem solving, handling discussions and teacher participation generally; and it helped me to gear my teaching to the needs of the individual children.

I believe that children learn best through enactive experiences, and the logical extension of this is that teachers do the same. I found two distinct advantages in action research: it enabled me to discover more about myself as a teacher, and I experienced a mode of learning I can incorporate into the work I plan for the children.

DAVID JACKSON

Food for thought

Asking questions about what happens in classrooms is as inevitable as breathing. Because this search for meaning in what we do is a basic human need we find teachers and pupils doing it all the time. Why has Tony been skulking in that corner for the last two weeks and why has he not done any work? Why do certain children fail at school? Why do some teachers allow talk in class and others do not? Why does the Thursday lesson always go wrong? Of course, some of these questions and speculations are slight, but others contain the first stirrings of important enquiries.

Teachers can usefully develop this natural skill in making sense of their own classroom experience. Outside observers may be able to offer fresh perspectives on and alternative interpretations of what goes on in the classroom, but teachers spend their working lives where the vital evidence must be sought. They know what it feels like to be on the inside of classrooms over long periods of time. They have the opportunities to tease out their own curiosities, questionings, reflections; to discover something of the significance of all that hectic busy-ness that goes on around them.

Some of the difficulties, and rewards, of trying to make sense of what happens in one's own classroom may be illustrated by my own attempts to record a second-year secondary class doing English. They were a mixed ability class of twenty-six 12 and 13 year olds working with me on the topic of 'Food'. In the following account I have juxtaposed against my description of what took place some retrospective comments written a few days later.

This second year class have already worked on whole-group

topics with me, like 'Monsters', 'Man and Creatures', 'Fun', 'Communication', 'Discoveries and Inventions', 'Friends and Enemies' and now 'Food'. The pupils are learning to negotiate with me about what they do and the way in which they do it in this classroom. I'm trying to convince them of the reality of a bargaining space that exists between their spontaneous interest, my enthusiasms, the resources and our physical environment. And they're mixed in their reaction; some are uncertain about what I'm trying to do and just want the comfortable routine of being told what to do and getting on with it, yet others make the topic their own with zest and good humour. Alison sits there looking perplexed, biting her fingernails, wanting me to tell her what to do and the way to go about it, while Helen's brimming over with ideas: 'Getting caught chewing gum in class. We could do a play on that.'

(I'm trying to talk about what went on in my classroom in a clearer, more explicit way so that other colleagues in other schools or institutions can share what I thought was going on. I agree; I'm tidying it up, organising it more neatly. Perhaps it would be more illuminating to have a pupil's and an observer's point of view as well, but this is a start isn't it?

I've tried to remain loyal to some of the uncertainty of the classroom. The intention was to tease out some of the complexities, the subtleties of tone.)

Initially the department developed individual worksheets for a mixed ability approach, but then reacted against the passive acceptance of them by many pupils. So now the thematic worksheets, collected in the departmental handbook, are ways of reminding and stimulating teachers of the possibilities surrounding various themes. I've just dipped into the 'Food' worksheet again and I'm bringing with me into the classroom remembered excitement about a poem by Adrian Mitchell called 'Deep Sherbet' from *The Apeman Cometh*, (Jonathan Cape):

> and when the sherbet
> hit the spittle
> on my palate –
> that's when the fizz began

Then there was the story by George Layton about the boy who makes aspic jelly, by mistake, for the school Christmas party ('All wobbly. But it was a bit of a funny colour – sort of yellowy – white') from *Northern Childhood: The Balaclava Story*, the Pete Burkis Special from *The Midnight Fox* ('. . . our mouths were on fire and cheese and sausage juice was dripping down our chins'), the terrible necessity to eat all the seventeen oranges in the Bill Naughton story and the firm clarity of the description of Nick eating out of doors in Hemingway's 'Big Two-Hearted River'.

(The choice of style is really important. I've always been an admirer of Connie Rosen's 'object lesson' voice,[1] crisp, direct, clear. Must make an effort here not to over-do the '. . . as so-and-so says', but try and say it how I experienced it. There's a place for quotation if it clarifies the argument but not just to give a false respectability.)

And also memories from my own childhood; of how important liquorice was to me at that age and the intensity of my reactions to my first school dinner. All of these combined memories gave me the impetus to want to introduce the 'Food' theme to this second year group.

(Why does the word 'anecdote' have to carry superficial, impressionistic connotations? Surely we need to dignify the anecdote and demonstrate its quality in giving heightened meaning to the process of reflection and generalisation?)

But where we met (teacher and pupils) was in some ways disappointing. We met every Wednesday afternoon in an open House area and the echoey, often dismal surroundings (especially after a wet dinner time) were made worse by the lack of safe display space and the straggles of children who came through this area from other lessons on their way to the toilet often breaking the group's concentration.

However there was greater scope for those activities that can take quite a bit of organising in the usual classroom box, like improvised drama and small group talk. So we got on with it and made the best of a bad job, but not before I had cleared up every scrap of crumpled paper and every overturned chair before the start of each lesson.

(If reports from inside one classroom are going to be credible to other teachers and interested readers then a more open and honest representation is needed. A fallible approach has probably got more chance of being believed in. Over-sterilised accounts can tend to widen the gap between the formal, academic research community removing their evidence from specific contexts and encounters, and teachers and pupils who hold different intentions and perceptions.

Perhaps practising teachers are only going to take on the unfamiliar (theoretical insights about what they're doing) through the familiar (everyday classroom realities)?)

The most difficult thing to get right in any classroom is the delicate equilibrium between the teacher's direction and the pupil's individual choice. Without the right preparation and careful training far too much children's work becomes disappointingly slack and stereotyped when they are given something approaching open choice. So the important thing in the first year was through a whole-class approach to engage their interest, make them enjoy English and to suggest a wide range of possibilities open to them and then to gradually train them up to take informed individual choices later on. And this is what I was trying to do with this second-year group.

I made it clear that our approach to this topic would be a balance between their ideas and my ideas. After chatting with the group about the possibilities within the Food topic (mostly taken from the teacher's thematic worksheet) I asked them to write down ten ideas of their own that they would like to do and told them that I would float in my ideas as a range of flexible options during the course of the topic. I stressed that it was no good putting the idea down without careful thought about the kind of activity that was going to convey the idea. For example whether they were going to make the idea into a play, radio script, series of letters, diary, journal, argument, short story, cartoon, poem, advertisement, or drawing. And I also drew attention to the need for a balanced spread of activities in their suggestions. (I didn't want anyone just handing in a book full of cartoons at the end of the topic.)

(The encouraging thing, I suppose, about keeping a journal on what

*you think is happening in your classroom, or regularly talking it
through, is the way you find you can learn more about what was going
on through the acts of writing and talking. Through sifting, selecting
and organising all those random impressions of the normal classroom
into a more coherent and carefully considered form, there's an intellectual sorting out going on. As well as exchanging your experiences
you're articulating the significance of what that activity meant to you.
The problem, of course, in looking for general patterns of meaning after
the event is that there is a tendency for the complexities of the actual
encounter to get lost.*

*Here, I'm able to focus my attention on a unifying theme: the nature
of the interaction between the pupils' initiatives and the teacher's
directions.)*

These are the ideas that two of the class produced; most of
them forgot my advice on activities:

IDEAS:

1. The splattered bubble: Write a descriptive passage or a
   poem.
2. Eating sweets in class: Do a play.
3. When you eat too much and you feel you could burst:
   Write a poem.
4. Make up a witches gruel recipe.
5. Write a story about the worlds cooking contest.
6. Write a letter to the head cook complaining about school
   dinners and write the reply.
7. Hunger.
8. Space food.
9. Write a menu for very thin people.
10. Draw an advertisement for a breakfast cereal.
11. Draw a knicker bocker glory.

                                                     MICHELE

TEN IDEAS

1. My favorite food.
2. A posh menu.
3. Draw a sandwich with different fillings.
4. Sucking sweets in class.

5. School dinners.
6. Make up an advert for advertising some sort of food.
7. The food I hate (poem).
8. Being a dinner moniter.
9. Children from the dinner ladies point of view.
10. 5 ways to tell if its powdered mash.

DEBBIE

School dinner was a source of constant involvement during the topic, and after talking to Debbie about some of the recent changes in the quality of school food she explored in her own way one of her ten ideas. I've chosen Debbie because, in many ways, her response to what we did was more independent than many in the form. The obvious danger is that I'm only selecting the most promising work.

. . . 5 . . . WAYS . . . TO . . . TELL . . . IF . . . ITS . . . POWDERED . . . MASH . . .

1. Eat it (but this is not advised unless you want to get indigestion).
2. Carefully dig through it with a knife. If it is bitty yellow this will prove its powdered.
3. Put it in your pocket. If it hasn't dissolved in 3 days you've got real potatoe. You've also got a very messy pocket oh well better luck nextime.
4. Smell it.
5. If you still can't tell here's one last resort listen to it, yes listen to it you can always tell powdered mash by the gurgles and burps.

At the end of the topic [the next week] I invited the whole group to comment on the topic and our way of working. These are some of the more interesting ones:

1. Honestly I think this topic was rotten it is downright boring, it is probably because I like writing adventure stories and there isn't many you can write about food.
   I think topics are alright but it would be better if we could choose our own.

2. I think the topic on food is good and I like the way we do it. It is good the way we do the plays and the topic.

3. It thought that the food topic was alright I like to right things about animals and do folders. I don't like writing 10 ideas in our books.

4. When we started this food topic I thought it was going to be good and I was right. I like the way we do it as a topic in our books but I don't like having folders. I don't like doing the teachers idea's I do like doing my own.

5. I think the food topic is okay it was not the best one we've done and I don't really like that sort of thing it got a bit boring, and its not like English. I liked some writing we did but like I said again it was a bit boring.

   I would rather do a Horror topic than Food but I think we should have a choose of say 4 topics like eg

   Horror topic
   Laugh topic
   Human topic
   Sea topic

   and we can choose which one of these ones we like.

6. I enjoyed most of the topic on food quite a lot because it had room for a lot of scope. I think we just had the right amount of time on it if we had had any more time on it I would have grown sick of it.

   I would like to work in a different way from this though sometimes say 1 topic lasting 2 weeks then if you didn't like it you weren't stuck on it for ages and ages as we were on communication.

It seems to me that many conventional research accounts of classrooms are out of touch with children and their spontaneous use of language when they feel valued. As well as giving a greater sense of authenticity the freshness and immediacy of details like 'bitty yellow' and 'gurgles and burps', from Debbie's piece on detecting powdered mash, often stand a greater chance of engaging the reader's attention than a more formal, abstract account. This is one reason why children's voices need to be given greater space. Also, many descriptions of classroom experience leave out children's perceptions of what's going on. Through contrasting their own versions with children's comments (as above), teachers can often learn more about the reasons behind classroom failures and successes.

The other reason brings in the particular theory of knowledge and of learning implied by this type of exploration. The pupils weren't just told what to do, although in a few cases they wanted the reassuring security of that kind of relationship with the teacher, but were invited to actively reconstruct the knowledge that was being used in that classroom through the participation between teacher and child. This explains some of the reasons behind the pupils' lists of ideas.

If 'what is known must in fact be brought to life afresh in every "knower" by his own efforts' (Bullock Report), then we have got to work out a new way of working with children in the classroom and also respecting what the child is bringing into the classroom in terms of everyday intuition and knowledge. Only if the child enters into the re-shaping of what is knowledge in that classroom will she/he be able to make unfamiliar, school knowledge personally meaningful to herself in that position.

This means, in practice, that the topic 'Food' as seen by the teacher is re-interpreted by the pupils in a different light. So that Debbie, because she is encouraged to bring her own everyday concerns about eating dinner in the school canteen into the classroom, is able to see that the 'Food' topic can mean thoughts about the difference between real potatoes and powdered mash, rather than poems about eating sherbet.

It is a pity that children's evaluative descriptions of classroom experience are often neglected. By writing their own comments on a topic and adopting a collaborative style of learning pupils have a chance to give an 'on the receiving end' version of what happened that often works as a frank and sobering corrective to teachers' rosier accounts.

'Honestly I think this topic was rotten . . .'
'I don't like writing ten ideas in our books.'
'I don't like doing the teacher's ideas. I do like doing my own.'
'I would like to work in a different way from this though . . .'

The gruff resistance of quite a few of these comments can be too easily labelled as negative catch-phrases. Initially, the pupils may have been puzzled at the comparative strangeness of some of the activities and suspicious of the teacher's motives. Gradually, however, they learnt that, by working in this way, they could have a greater say in what they did and in the way in which they did it. Their involvement in the task of evaluation sharpened both their own and their teacher's understanding of the class-room experience.

So what about the difficulties and rewards of this kind of approach? Clearly it does take considerable time and energy, but it can make teachers more effective in their classroom practice. Through the reflective acts of talking and writing (e.g. keeping a regular journal; being a little more systematic about organising small group talk) about what they think happened, teachers can become more consciously aware of why children, and they themselves, do the things they do.

In trying to focus attention on the quality of teacher/child encounter, teachers might find that they discover more about how to concentrate their limited energies on central learning priorities rather than rushing around in a randomly haphazard way. They also might find that they are moving into a position where they can organise the classroom context and choose their own teaching style with more consideration and coherence.

And, finally, this kind of approach often brings with it a boost to personal confidence in an increasingly demoralised climate. Really taking control of and caring about the quality of what is going on in your classroom leads some teachers into seeing themselves as active initiators rather than child managers. With this shift in self-image there sometimes goes a developing sense of power and positive self-esteem, in being able to become more professional about one's job through one's own efforts rather than relying on other educational agencies – inspectors, academic researchers, etc – to say what ought to be done.

REFERENCES

1. In Jones, A. & Mulford, J. (eds), *Children Using Language: an approach to English in the Primary School*, OUP, 1972.

DAVID GOWER

The chemistry of the classroom

When I joined the staff of a new comprehensive school in the
Autumn of 1976, it was with a certain sense of adventure. The
school had been open for only two previous years, so the boys
and girls from the original intake were just starting their third
year of secondary education. Unhampered by previous structures or traditions, the staff were free to develop a curriculum in
accordance with what they believed to be the best of contemporary educational thinking. Money was available in those
pre-spending-cut days, the staff enthusiastic and committed.

For its academic organisation, the school was based on a
faculty system whereby the curriculum was divided into six
subject areas. Every student was expected to take courses in each
faculty during his or her first five years at school. Such a 'core'
system avoided problems of premature specialisation and conse-
quent career limitations. It did, however, impose the problem of
devising course material suitable for the full secondary age and
ability range.

I took on the task of designing science courses. Science
comprised the disciplines of Biology, Chemistry and Physics
plus any Rural Science, Geology, Astronomy etc., that we saw
fit to introduce. For the first to third years we adopted complete
mixed ability teaching of Integrated Science. In the fourth and
fifth years we divided our students into two groups taking 'O'
Level (double certificate) and six further parallel groups taking
CSE (double certificate). We looked for course material which
was relevant to our students' everyday lives, was intrinsically
interesting and that led to recognised science qualifications for
future jobs or further education. The situation led constantly to
basic questions: What to teach? To whom? In what sequence?
How to assess the learning that resulted? Some of these are

questions that every thoughtful teacher must ask and can also
begin to answer through research in his or her own classroom.

I needed information about planning classroom learning: the
selection, structuring and sequencing of material for the science
education of a thousand children. There was plenty to look at by
way of published material, though much of this was designed
for more able children taking traditional separate science subjects
rather than for a situation in which all students spent 20 per cent
of their time taking science. Available material ranged from
curriculum projects by the Nuffield Foundation and the Schools
Council to text books from the avant garde to the avowedly
traditional. Examination syllabuses and consultations with other
schools soon gave an impression of the norm for comprehensive
school science.

The teacher is almost like a child in the supermarket, tempted
to choose the newest or most brightly coloured packages or, if
more cautious, to look and see what most other customers seem
to select. Suppose, however, something better is looked for. In
the interest of doing the best we can for the children we teach,
what rationale should lie behind our selection? Can we pick and
choose at will in accordance with our experience or professional
prejudices? Will our students be educationally damaged if we
make the wrong choices, however good our motives? What
information does the teacher need to turn from being a speculative shopper in the curriculum supermarket to becoming an
informed consumer? Is this in itself not a potentially fruitful field
for teacher research?

Science teaching has changed appreciably in the past ten to
fifteen years. It is relevant here to consider the rationale behind
the changes, so that classroom research into the success of
various kinds of course material can be seen in its proper
perspective.

Traditionally, subjects such as Chemistry and Mathematics
were included in the curriculum on the basis that they were
difficult subjects which would exercise students' minds. By
performing complicated exercises in calculations or through
learning the products and conditions for numerous chemical
reactions, the faculties of 'reasoning' and 'memory' respectively

would develop. If learning is an exercise in training the mind, then, so the argument ran, the harder the material, the better. Traditional curricula emphasise the acquisition of wide knowledge as evidence of subject mastery. The memorising of facts, either to develop the memory faculty or because the facts themselves are viewed as an essential ingredient of a subject, is a primary aim of traditional teaching. There is some evidence that 'learning' is almost synonymous in the popular mind with 'remembering information'. (Perhaps 'Data Bank of Britain' would be a more appropriate title than 'Brain of Britain' for the radio series.)

Experimental psychology overturned the traditional mental exercise theory by showing that one memory exercise (e.g. learning French irregular verbs) did not produce any corresponding improvement in another (e.g. learning lists of chemical symbols) as one would expect if the earlier learning had developed the memory faculty. More recent research has shown that 'transfer' (a student's ability to apply to a new situation material learned in a different situation) depends on both the kind of material and how it is taught. First, the *method* employed by a learner to solve a problem is transferable to other situations. This demands understanding of the material, not mere rote memorising. Secondly, it appears that the more generalised the information learned, the greater the possibilities of transfer.

The volume of contemporary scientific knowledge is so immense that one individual during his lifetime can hope to know only a small part. This explosion of knowledge has been responsible for ever-increasing school syllabuses, a serious situation which has been partially resolved by changing the way in which Science is presented. Educational philosophers have represented the different academic disciplines as different ways of knowing. It can be argued from this that a complete education should involve each discipline – part of the justification for a 'core curriculum' rather than an option system in a secondary school.

If students study all disciplines, this can only be achieved by in-depth study, for any superficial approach would fail to communicate the essential inner logic of each subject. Thus a

characteristic 'new-type' Science syllabus such as SCISP contains a rather restricted range of information and is confined to
fewer areas of a subject than would be the case with more
traditional schemes of work. This leads to the formation of
broad generalisations within the area studied, rather than the
acquisition of isolated facts about a much wider field.

So philosophical and psychological arguments brought about
syllabus revision in Science, leading to material which was
abstract and general rather than simply factual and which
demanded understanding on the part of the learner rather than
memorisation. The 'new' courses were also characterised by an
emphasis on individual student practical work. Discovery learning results in greater transfer of learning to new situations
because the student discovers for himself techniques for learning
new generalisations. It was argued that only by 'being a scientist'
could a student come to understand Science as a process of
inquiry.

So back to the 'curriculum supermarket'. In attempting to
select suitable books and structure course material, the teacher
could be guided by the following philosophical and psychological principles which underlie current thinking in Science
courses:

A. Science is viewed as a process of enquiry rather than as a
   body of knowledge to be learned.
B. The subject matter is organised into a logical pattern in a
   form which stresses broad generalisations rather than
   specific details.
C. The courses are structured so that the learner himself can
   discover broad generalisations and hence 'learn how to
   learn'.
D. The courses demand that the student understands the
   material rather than merely remembering it. He is required
   to show evidence of his understanding by solving problems. Some emphasis is placed on individual creativity
   since many of the problems have an unfamiliar context and
   no prescribed method for solution.

The teacher might reasonably expect to be able to draw on

experimental evidence on the relationship between a student's mental ability and the level of generalisation and abstraction with which he can cope. However, there is a notable dearth of such research. Lacking this information, it would be all too easy to devise courses which adhered to the principles listed above but which were beyond the capabilities of the people for whom they were intended. To devise the right courses requires:

A. Knowledge of the detailed structure of Science in a form that can be applied to curriculum development, and

B. Detailed information concerning the stages of concept formation in children's thinking.

The central question is, 'At what ages or stages in development are certain topics or skills most effectively or efficiently taught?' It is my contention that this is an area in which the teacher-researcher can function most effectively. It involves assessing children's success at coping with their work and pinpointing causes of failure. It also involves the teacher in acquiring sufficient skills in research and educational assessment to be able to carry out meaningful experiments and draw valid conclusions.

I began my own career by teaching Chemistry to well-motivated and, on the whole, intelligent children. Like many teachers, I became concerned for those students who were anxious to succeed in the subject, but failed even though they obviously tried hard. I began to wonder why some topics in the revised Chemistry syllabuses were notoriously difficult. I tried talking to colleagues, reading teacher-based publications and talking to the students themselves, but discovered little beyond the fact that the failure of hard-working students is part of every teacher's professional experience. Feeling that some more organised approach was called for, I registered at Bath University for a part-time M Ed (research) degree.[2] I aimed to construct tests of depth of understanding of some basic chemical concepts, intending thereby to analyse in some detail my students' progress in some of the problem areas in school Chemistry. Without the experienced supervision of the university staff at Bath, the research could never have been achieved, even though most of it reflects my own thinking and reading and was carried out in my own classroom. The kind of study I wanted to pursue involved a good working knowledge of educational test construction and statistical analysis. These are not usually part of initial teacher-training and must therefore be learned subsequently by the teacher-researcher. I set out in my own research to analyse part of the 'O' Level Chemistry syllabus which students seemed to find particularly difficult.

Understanding Chemistry (or any other subject for that matter) requires understanding of its basic concepts. 'Concept' is a psychological term describing a person's readiness to respond to particular stimuli in the same way. This can be illustrated by an example: presented with a strange object, a person tries to classify it in terms of something familiar – 'a sort of fruit' for instance. The concept 'fruit' is a very generalised one, comprising objects as different as pears, pineapples and bananas but having something in common which is expressed by putting them into the same category. A concept is therefore a classification device, defined in terms of the attributes which all members of a class have in common. By thinking in terms of concepts rather than isolated, specific items of information, we are able to generalise, compare and think abstractly. Concepts represent the ways in which an individual has organised his past experience and in terms of which he is able to interpret new material to be learned. So concepts are the means whereby previous learning is applied to new situations.

Some concepts will only be meaningful to a student if he has first mastered others. Consider the following sequence:

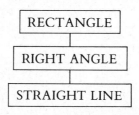

The concept 'rectangle' depends on the prior understanding of 'right angle' which is itself meaningless to a student who has not understood the concept of a 'straight line'.

This method of analysis is derived from the work of Robert Gagné. At each stage the teacher asks the question, 'What must the students have previously understood before they can understand the ideas with which I want to present them now?' The resulting 'learning hierarchy' can be displayed as a flow chart. It indicates to the teacher that *students will fail* to learn what he is teaching *unless* he has first successfully taught them *all* the subsidiary concepts.

The flow charts which can be produced from this kind of analysis can be complicated, branching structures.[3] Is this learning model a useful one? Do children actually learn according to the sequences it describes? I decided to test an area from the third-year Science programme which included the chemical ideas 'element', 'mixture' and 'compound'. Understanding of these concepts is essential for the understanding of most 'O' Level Chemistry syllabuses, modern or traditional. 'Elements, compounds and mixtures' could be so inextricably related that learning one is impossible without learning the others. This would imply that all three should be taught simultaneously. On the other hand, if the relationship is hierarchical, they might better be learned in a particular sequence, as shown in Figure 1.

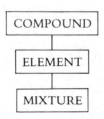

Figure 1. Learning hierarchy for three simple concepts

The experimental hypothesis was that students *cannot* understand the meaning of 'compound' without first understanding what is meant by an 'element'. This, in turn, depends on the concept 'mixture'.

Our first group of third year students at Hextable school consisted of some 180 boys and girls, covering the whole comprehensive ability range in a close approximation to a 'normal' distribution. Their course was taught by three different teachers, following the same detailed lesson-by-lesson plan through the course material. There was therefore some variation in the learning experiences of different forms as staff approached the material in their own ways while adhering to the overall plan. However, since the experiment was designed to test the hypothesis that learning *must* follow the hierarchical sequence, the variations in teaching tended to improve the experimental design. If a significant number of children succeeded in learning the three concepts in some order other than the one suggested, the hypothesis would be invalidated, no matter how they achieved this.

At the end of the course unit all students took a multiple choice test which included items specially written to test understanding of the three concepts. These were not easy to produce, since 'understanding', not memory, was to be tested. It was necessary first to learn the skills required for the production of technically sound good multiple choice items. A panel of experts (teachers in schools and universities) scrutinised the items to check their validity (that is, that they tested the skills and knowledge they were supposed to test). Unsuccessful items were re-written or scrapped. Particular care was taken to control variables such as language complexity which could influence the difficulty of items to the students.

Details of the statistical analysis applied appear in a paper on classroom research given to a symposium sponsored by the Chemical Society.[1] One way of looking at the results is in terms of the percentage of the students who were successful on the items dealing with each particular concept. These are given below together with the corresponding figures obtained from a similar experiment at a Bristol comprehensive school. The same items were used in both cases, but the Bristol children had not followed the same schemes of work. They were also older, fifth formers rather than third formers.

The results (shown in Figure 2) are consistent with the

Concept	Hextable	Bristol
Mixture	88	84
Element	64	49
Compound	39	47

Figure 2. Percentage of students successful on items dealing with the three concepts (161 students at Hextable, 43 in Bristol)

experimental hypothesis and stood up to more rigorous statistical treatment designed to determine how far the variation could be attributed to chance. In no sense is the hypothesis proved, but it does survive a test which suggests that further work along the same lines is likely to be profitable. In the absence of further evidence, courses that follow a hierarchical sequence are likely to benefit the students, if only through the amount of rigorous preparation in which they will have involved the teacher.

Perhaps the greatest advantage that a teacher-researcher has in this kind of work lies in his sensitivity to classroom needs. To answer the question, 'What must my students understand before I can teach this piece of work?' requires thoughtful understanding of young people as well as detailed knowledge of one's subject. It is a task that the experienced teacher is well-qualified for, one in which he can make worthwhile contributions to subject teaching knowledge *provided* that he is also prepared to learn the necessary research skills.

To produce a learning hierarchy requires subject knowledge and expertise, teaching experience, patience and the ability to see one's subject from the perspective of the student. Take, for example the flow diagram of a hierarchy dealing with the formation of shadows (Figure 3). Each box represents a stage of development in the student's understanding in terms of the concepts he is expected to cope with. At the bottom of the diagram are two basic concepts which the child must first form from his own experience. Transparent/opaque is a simple categorisation of materials. The technical words in themselves are unimportant; what is required is that the child perceives the world in terms of materials he can see through and ones that he cannot. The second basic concept is that of light and darkness.

Darkness is the absence of light; the more light, the brighter the surroundings become.

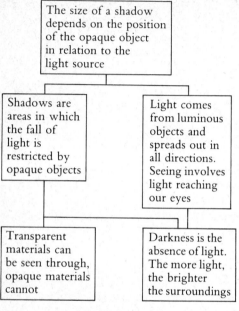

Figure 3.

The key to understanding how shadows are formed lies in the apparently simple idea that opaque objects block out light, causing the area behind them to be lit less brightly than its surroundings. The diagram shows this to be dependent on the two root concepts of transparent/opaque and light/darkness. Further understanding of the properties of shadows depends on a deeper knowledge of light. The diagram indicates the extra knowledge required as the idea that light from a luminous object spreads out in all directions in straight lines. Technically the terms 'point source' and 'cone of light rays' would describe this.

The flow diagram is a simplification; one section of a much larger map showing relations between basic ideas in optics. Read from the bottom upwards it charts a student's developing insights. Read from the top downwards it indicates what subsidiary ideas a student must master in order to reach an ultimate objective. The flow chart gives a 'knowledge map' of the teacher's objectives for the learner. It enables the teacher to plan sequences of lessons which will cover all the concepts a student needs to form en route to a particular objective and hence for teaching to be as economical and effective as possible.

It is interesting, in the analysis, to see the way in which the knowledge map for the learner differs from that of the subject expert. Each little step is an essential one for the learner, but some would be passed over by the subject expert as scarcely worthy of mention. Yet it is at these points that students can stumble. The knowledge maps put information in a form in which it can easily be scrutinised by other teachers, who can comment usefully on the validity from their own teaching experiences.

Knowledge maps, such as this, provide information vital to the curriculum designer in a simple format. Explicit knowledge of the subject structure can prevent him from missing out essential elements from the schemes he produces. By thus preventing a student from seeing all the links between the concepts which he learns, a faulty design may well hinder the student in building up as complete and generalisable picture as he could. In an extreme case this would make Science appear to the learner as a collection of haphazard ideas and facts, preventing generalisation and appreciation of Science as a process of enquiry. Only the more able students could fill in the gaps for themselves.

Children whose motivation is not very strong soon give up if the subject matter they are asked to learn is not meaningful to them. Meaningful learning occurs only when a student can slot the new material into place among previously learned ideas. If he cannot do this because he has not acquired the necessary subsidiary concepts he can try to remember information (rote learning) but cannot integrate it into his personal thought structure.

I began by describing the situation at a new comprehensive school where I had the task of designing Science courses. The approach we adopted follows the kind of sequencing strategies I have described, though we are a long way from having achieved a detailed analysis of every area of the subject. The philosophy, however, has also made itself felt in two other ways: in the field of assessment and in Applied Science.

Traditional 'O' Level and CSE Science courses tend to work with theoretical and laboratory examples of scientific principles and then to introduce everyday examples almost on a 'take it or leave it' basis. According to the hierarchical theory, however, meaningful learning should be easier to achieve if new material is related to knowledge which students have already conceptual-ised. Using everyday experience as a basis for a Science course is to build on familiar concepts. Thus we introduce combustion chemistry through 'fuels' and 'fire-prevention', work and ener-gy through their effects on the body, and so on. This also has the advantage of making Science seem relevant to the pupils' everyday concerns. By integrating theoretical ideas by using the same principles, we achieve a higher level of theoretical Science than many CSE Mode 1 courses demand.

We have adopted a 'modular' course both for 'O' Level and CSE as well as the first to third years. Each module comprises work on a section of the course and is described in lesson by lesson detail in a teachers' handbook. The modular approach is usefully flexible, allowing unsuccessful lessons or entire units to be rewritten with minimal disturbance to the rest of the course. It also lends itself to a system in which the objectives of a unit are stated at the beginning and a test based on those objectives is administered at the end. This is used to evaluate the students' learning and to indicate parts of the course on which they have been unsuccessful – as much a criticism of the teaching and the teacher as of the students. Testing is therefore essentially diagnostic.

The construction of diagnostic tests is a skilled exercise. It is part of my own research training that I have found of immense value in the classroom. Yet assessment techniques do not usually seem to form any significant part of initial teacher training. In consequence some horrifying statistical procedures survive in schools. Teachers still total and average marks from different tests and even different subjects and use the averages in coursework grades that may well affect students' lives, despite the fact that such a procedure is statistical nonsense. Some still set examinations which are little more than a collection of questions with no thought given to the intellectual skills being tested. They then compute percentages from the results and expect to make valid inferences about their students.

Our own tests are made up of questions with specific intentions; testing particular concepts and particular intellectual skills. A group of questions might, for example, test the ecological 'community' theme. Easier ones demand only comprehension (the ability to use the idea in familiar contexts). More demanding items test application (ability to use concepts in unfamiliar contexts or as abstractions), and the ability to analyse data or synthesis (creative problem solving). The higher the intellectual skill, the harder the problem. Such testing is sophisticated and takes a long while to devise. At Hextable we have scarcely begun the kind of diagnostic programme we should like to produce. Only through computerisation will we be able to provide as much help for our students as we should like. We are beginning to make progress in this field.

Once a teacher gets into the habit of thinking in terms of hierarchies, it makes him very sensitive to his students' learning. Often the solution to the situation in which a class have obviously not 'caught on' is greater structuring. Careful questioning of children who have got a problem wrong can establish the point in a hierarchy at which their understanding failed. Examination questions which are structured in a similar way allow for a more formal assessment. As he becomes more sensitive to children's thinking, so the teacher is less inclined to use unnecessary technical or other complex language in expressing his ideas, and puts each step simply, clearly and directly. The factors which combine to increase the difficulty of examination questions include intellectual skill (comprehension, application, etc.) and the position of a concept within a hierarchy (the higher the concept, the harder it is to acquire), as well as language complexity[4].

There is no reason why the kind of research I have carried out should be confined to Science. Material in other subjects, if meaningful learning is expected of the students, must be conceptual. If it is conceptual, it can be analysed in the same manner as I have begun to analyse Science courses. It seems to me that this is one kind of research that is valuable to teachers and that teachers can carry out themselves.

So, in the curriculum supermarket, the teacher need not be taken in by the packaging nor bewildered by the variety of goods on display. Many would argue that the transition from speculative shopper to informed consumer is the product of experience in the classroom and that there is no short cut to professional maturity. It is, however, the quality of our experience which determines the depth of our maturity. The teacher who actively attempts to analyse his students' learning difficulties, to structure his courses accordingly and to share the results of his research with his colleagues profits from a different kind of experience from the teacher who sees maturity in terms of class control and examination results.

REFERENCES

1. Gower, D. M. & Daniels, D. J., 'The Hierarchical Structure of O-level Chemistry', in *Research for the Classroom and Beyond: A Report of a Symposium*, The Chemical Society, 1977.
2. Gower, D. M., *Conceptual Difficulty in Chemistry: The Mole Concept*, Unpublished M Ed thesis: University of Bath, 1975.
3. Gower, D. M., Daniels, D. J. & Lloyd, G., 'The Mole Concept', *School Science Review*, 1977, *58* (205), 658–76; and 'Hierarchies among the concepts which underlie the mole', *School Science Review*, 1977, **59** (207), 285–99.
4. Gower, D. M. & Daniels, D. J., 'Some factors which influence the facility value of objective test items in school chemistry', *Studies in Educational Evaluation*, 1980, **6,** 127–36.

Pointers: 1

* This section has dealt in some detail with a few of the ways in which teachers can document their own lessons. A less detailed but more comprehensive outline of research techniques is available in the Ford Teaching Project booklet, *Ways of doing research in one's own classroom* (see Appendix).

* How can the teacher ensure that comments elicited from pupils, either in interview or by questionnaire, are an honest expression of their opinions?

* Initially it may be necessary for the teacher as researcher to focus on a narrow area of enquiry. More can be learnt from a detailed analysis of one child's paintings than from a cursory review of the art work of a whole class.

* There are a number of duties which teachers have to perform on a regular basis. These include marking attendance registers, setting achievement tests and marking pupils' written work. It might be worth considering whether there are any ways in which these routine activities could profitably be treated as research tasks. Several of the chapters in Marten Shipman's *In-School Evaluation* might prove useful in this respect (see Appendix).

* When developing a research method it may be necessary to use a variety of techniques. Pupil interviews and observation notes, for example, are valuable ways of cross-checking the teacher's own field notes.

* A teacher's work load varies throughout the year according to

the school's report cycle and the timing of the public examinations. It is important that teachers about to embark on
classroom research should be aware of the pattern of their
own commitments. The first priority is to find a method
which works within the constraints of the school day.

2

School concerns

JON NIXON

School concerns

Teachers adopting a research stance to their work cannot go it alone. They require the goodwill of colleagues and the moral and practical support of senior staff. The first chapter in this section concentrates on the problems of carrying out research within one's own school. The other three chapters represent a variety of ways in which teachers in different schools have tried to overcome these problems by involving a greater number of staff in the research process. One teacher forged an important link with a colleague in a neighbouring school; another participated in a departmental approach to action research; while the last chapter describes an attempt to develop the school as a self-evaluating community. Each of the authors is concerned with the question of how existing relations and structures within the school can be utilised in implementing school based research. As with the last section the strategies outlined in the following pages should not be seen as universally applicable. Each was tailored to the needs of a particular situation. Nevertheless, taken together they represent a serious attempt to broaden the base of action research so as to strengthen its position within the school structure.

Ensuring that one's research is tailored to the needs of a particular situation involves the teacher in a number of initial procedures: consultation, negotiation and planning.

1. Before starting the research, sources both inside and outside the school should be consulted. There may be teachers working in the school who have experience in action research; their expertise should be drawn on. Advisory teachers, Teachers' Centre wardens and higher education personnel may also have useful comments to make. What is

important is that the teacher finds interested and experienced people with whom to discuss the research and the way in which it is to be implemented.

2. In almost all school-based research some negotiation is necessary with colleagues and senior staff. As a point of principle this negotiation should involve all who are in any way effected by the research. These may be limited to members of one's own department. They may, however, include a much wider cross-section of the staff, in which case the matter would probably need to be raised at a full staff meeting. Although this procedure may seem time-consuming, it serves to create a more informed atmosphere within which to carry out one's research.

3. It is a mistake to think that all one's planning should be done on paper. Where one's research involves working alongside other teachers in the classroom it may be necessary to try out a variety of approaches before settling on the most effective one. This is certainly the case with classroom observation. Teacher and observer should each give the other time to become relaxed and confident in their presence. Easy collaboration can only be achieved through the experience of working together in the classroom so that agreement can be reached on the rights and responsibilities of each member of the team.

MARY JAMES AND DAVE EBBUTT

Problems and potential

This chapter examines the issues which confront a teacher in conducting research in his or her school. It is derived from our own experiences, as full-time teachers, of carrying out a programme of research in our schools. In the account which follows we have described issues in the chronological sequence in which they arose, or at least came to prominence. This is not to say that they were characteristic of any phase in the research process. Many, like the problems associated with the adoption of a research role, were with us most of the time. However, we decided on a roughly chronological structure because we thought others might more easily recognise the issues. We will of course make reference to the strategies which we employed to overcome the problems we encountered, in the hope that this will make the process easier for others. The strategies we mention are in no way prescriptive; they merely helped towards a resolution of some of our problems.

We both recognise that personal history and extrinsic incentive motivated our research. One of us (DE) had been involved with the Ford Teaching Project and was connected with the Cambridge Institute of Education and the Classroom Action Research Network (CARN). The other (MJ), whilst lacking any background in action research, had taught the Humanities Curriculum Project and Sociology, and had developed an interest in social research generally and the experimental approach to classrooms in particular. Moreover we had both embarked on MAs in Curriculum Studies and we hoped that an attempt at insider research might fulfil the dissertation requirements as well as providing us with some practical insights into our everyday teaching.

Although we have come to regard action research as an

integral part of the teacher's role, we think it is unrealistic to expect all teachers to be any more altruistic than we were. The teacher who adopts a researcher stance is still an innovator. In the absence of 'carrots' or 'sticks', such as we had, it is not really surprising that many teachers consider school-based research an optional extra, to be engaged in if and when other commitments allow.

MJ's difficulty in introducing and gaining acceptance for what amounted to an innovation in her school created a need for support from a group such as that which already existed for DE. Contacts made on the MA course formed the core of this group. Our experience suggests that the motivation to begin and sustain teacher research depends significantly on contacts with others engaged in this kind of work, whether they assume a role of 'expert' supervisor, sponsor, consultant, collaborator or 'critical friend'. For those currently lacking the contacts that we developed, supportive networks do exist: the Classroom Action Research Network is one, and the Schools Council is giving serious consideration to sponsoring/supporting others (see Appendix).

In our experience, however, this kind of support is not sufficient. The teacher who attempts research in his own classroom or school without some support from his colleagues is likely to encounter difficulties. Often sympathetic understanding and encouragement is all that is required, but this is not always forthcoming. Even research confined to one's own classroom is sometimes interpreted as threatening by others. For example, MJ was charged by a colleague and friend with undermining her own professional status and, by implication, that of her colleagues. By looking at her own practice so openly was not MJ publicly confessing to her own shortcomings, and was not this likely to lower the image of the profession? On another occasion, MJ's practice of interviewing pupils to obtain feedback on her own lessons had apparently encouraged pupils to volunteer criticism to other teachers who were unprepared for such a response, negative or otherwise.

Thus we have come to regard the creation of an environment which is conducive to research as crucial. In many schools this atmosphere has to be created by the teacher-researchers themselves. It is clearly best, rather than being secretive, to let colleagues (and pupils if they are directly involved) know what is being done, and why. The channels for such communication will vary from school to school. Staff meetings may provide opportunities, although we found informal conversations with individuals to be perhaps the most productive.

Sometimes, of course, more practical support is needed. We found it helpful, and probably essential, for the Head and those above us in the hierarchy to support the research, for instance, by giving access to certain kinds of data and making available a certain amount of research time.

In all these cases we feel that the teacher-researcher needs to be prepared to be very tactful with colleagues. However, it would be misleading to suggest that we established general support for our research activities. For example, MJ circulated a questionnaire to 68 staff in the school and received only ten responses. We both encountered apathy and scepticism from some of our colleagues, although never active resistance.

With regard to choosing a focus for research, we both formulated a number of questions which had been in our minds for some time. This was not difficult. What was more of a problem was deciding what could reasonably be investigated within the constraints of the particular situation, and what the bounds of the enquiry should be. Perhaps the greatest danger was in simply attempting too much. The selection of a manageable area for investigation was vital. By manageable we mean capable of being investigated without making unjustifiable inroads into teaching commitments, and equally importantly, maintaining bounds around one's spare time. We both found this difficult. Whilst DE had a clearly focused research area (aspects of why girls are 'turned off' by physical science), early thoughts in terms of an explanation would have involved writing a sociology of the entire locality. The question only became manageable when it was decided that explanations should be sought within the school only.

Meanwhile MJ had chosen to look at what effects the teaching of courses geared towards social understanding had on the consciousness of pupils, teachers and parents. Immediately she was confronted by numerous choices. What kind of courses could she look at? Sociology, social economics, social studies, social education and humanities courses, at GCE, CSE and non-examination level, all existed in the school. What aspects of consciousness should she explore: knowledge, feelings, attitudes or values? What groups of pupils, which teachers, and who else would be the subjects of enquiry? She decided to look at fifth-year pupils taking 'O' Level Sociology and CSE Social Studies, mainly in her own classes. She focused particularly on social understanding and social attitudes, and compared pupils' perceptions and evaluations with those of specialist and non-specialist teachers and parents.

In the light of our experience we would strongly advocate a little, to be studied in some depth. 'Small is beautiful' in this type of endeavour. Inevitably there are areas that any researcher neglects, and questions are raised in the course of the work which cannot all be pursued immediately. However, by setting a fairly circumscribed goal the teacher is more likely to reach it, produce a report and thereby create the confidence to continue.

In retrospect it seems to us there are two main obstacles to getting started: not knowing what to do, and not having enough confidence to begin. For MJ, with no previous involvement in practical research, this proved almost paralysing. She felt this was exacerbated by her realisation that her knowledge of social science theory and methodology was incomplete, and her belief that others expected research 'purity', if the 'findings' were to be at all credible. This resulted in a desire to learn everything about various perspectives, in the conviction that nothing should be attempted until all theory was assimilated. She would still be reading now, if deadlines and a bit of direction from the course supervisor together with DE had not intervened. They advised identifying a few issues from informal interviews. On reflection this was the obvious approach, for it suited her interests and aptitudes.

For DE the second obstacle was more of a hindrance, but in

essence the same technique was employed to overcome it. By asking children if they would co-operate in an investigation which would involve them in such activities as taped whole-class discussion, or taped individual or group interviews, or in answering questionnaires, an expectation was set up in their minds. Having set it up, then the stimulus to begin actually came from the pupils: the researcher was obliged to start, to arrange interviews in response to the clamour from pupils. Feelings of self-consciousness over carrying a tape recorder everywhere soon disappeared and eventually such procedures became second nature. For reasons which will be explored later, the gathering of staff perceptions was a little more difficult to initiate.

We both gave considerable thought to the ethics of our proposed research, although at this time ethical questions and decisions about method and technique were somewhat inter-twined. If we were to use taped unstructured interviews of both staff and pupils, what rights of confidentiality and control over interview material should informants retain? Should staff and pupils be quoted anonymously in a final report? Our initial thoughts were that all respondents should be anonymised and that all should have total control over their data. We did not consider the question of parental permission to interview children. As the research progressed, minor events occurred which we had not anticipated and this caused us to rethink and amplify our ethical position; we found that no amount of forethought can envisage the inherent messiness of the develop-ing situation. This is an important point: but the researcher should not be deterred by it.

Once pupil interviews and discussions were underway it became important in DE's case to check their perceptions against those of the teaching staff. The staff were approached hesitantly and gently during normal staffroom conversations. The approach involved a request for a form list here, or a mark list there, in fact for bits of factual information which teachers usually have to hand anyway. Alternatively, the approach involved a request for colleagues to lend their special skills to the research; for example, a skilled and talented photographer

willingly photographed an interesting example of children's
work. From these initiatives it was still a big step to request 'an
interview' with a person who had been a colleague for nine
years, but these small initiatives fitted such a request into
context. Such strategies were felt to be necessary because of the
conflict of roles which the researcher encounters.

We hesitate to advocate only one methodological approach to
insider research. The choice needs to take into consideration the
nature of the research problem and the skills of the researcher.
However, our personal preference was for qualitative or quasi-
statistical techniques.[1] Our reasons were various. Some were
connected with the degree of statistical sophistication required to
make valid and reliable quantitative comparisons. Others more
directly concerned the economy of the research task. This is the
'manageable bounds' issue once more. We were interested in
school-based research because it offered us an opportunity to
look at our own classrooms, departments or schools with a view
to diagnosing problems and finding means to improve practice.
We decided that rigorous comparative measures were unlikely
to repay the amount of effort needed to develop them. For us,
qualitative methods such as informal interviews, participant
observation, open-ended questionnaires, photographs, diaries
and original documents provided a rich yet manageable source
of data.

   Having chosen a field of enquiry and a suitable range of
investigative techniques, the next problem was gaining access to
the potential sources of information: both people (pupils,
teachers, parents) and events (lessons, meetings). The teacher-
researcher already has a role within the school; we found this
almost inevitably affected access to data. The problem of
obtaining 'honest' feedback arose for us at this point. For
instance it was likely that pupils, particularly, found it difficult
to separate the researcher role from the teacher role. If they
perceived the teacher-researcher as 'having authority' they may
have sought to give answers to questions that they believed to be
'correct' in terms of their usual expectations of what a teacher
wants, rather than 'true' in terms of their own feelings and

perceptions. MJ asked some of her pupils whether the fact that she, their teacher, was interviewing them constrained their answers. She soon abandoned this line of questioning as she quickly realised that if they answered in the negative it would be equally plausible to infer that their answers were actually affirmative! However, the constructive outcome of this was that since the pupils knew that MJ shared with them a specialised language and set of concepts, and certain classroom experiences, they felt free to draw on these in answering questions. They suggested that they might have felt constrained had they not known the background of their interviewer. We feel that many of the seeming disadvantages of the teacher-researcher's dual role can be offset by making the most of shared experiences and established relationships. Probably much the same obtains when the co-operation of other teachers is sought, although here, too, perceptions of role and status can be intrusive.

In schools information can be passed up the hierarchy fairly easily. Thus as Heads of Department we had little difficulty gathering data from children; however, tension increased as we requested information from those above us. To get the free flow of information downwards seems almost to be against the gravitational laws of institutions. For example, MJ found it considerably more difficult to arrange interviews with those above her in the status hierarchy, than with either pupils or immediate colleagues. In the end the Head was interviewed at eight o'clock one morning as this was the only time made available to her. Significantly, this was the only occasion when she chose not to negotiate the use of a tape recorder. Efforts to arrange an interview with a deputy head were even less successful. In the end notes were written based on conversations reconstructed from the past which were then passed back for comment. In fact this strategy elicited a very interesting written response which shed considerable light on her view of the place of Social Studies in the whole curriculum. In particular, she seemed to have a low opinion of sociology because she had a low opinion of social workers.

The role of the Head was crucial. An illustration of this occurred when MJ wanted to find out about the views of parents. The Head was obviously concerned to have sight of all communication with the world outside the school, but having been consulted at an early stage and having cleared the question-naire, he took no further part. DE, however, was not allowed by his Head to pin some observations on the staffroom notice board, in order to stimulate discussion, because the room was used by evening centre staff.

We would like at this point to return to the problems of our ethical position as teacher-researchers. One may argue that giving some control over the research process to participants will result in data loss, if not distortion. We would agree, but feel that in some circumstances ethical considerations must be allowed to override the desire to retain and use all the data we are able to collect. A particular problem is posed for the teacher-researcher in that he has access to a constant flow of data merely by being always present in the school. Further, whilst pupils and colleagues may be aware that a teacher is engaged in research, they may divulge things to him 'as a teacher' that they would not want noted by him 'as a researcher'. How is the teacher-researcher to know which role he is perceived to have at any one time and how is he to handle the resulting data? This is not a problem that we felt we resolved to our total satisfaction. As a general rule, we only used data that we collected with the full cognisance and agreement of participants, although MJ recalls using as evidence at least one small but significant remark that was undoubtedly directed to her 'as a teacher' before her research properly began.

Mostly, data was only collected after the participants had been informed of the purposes of the research. Once collected their agreement was sought regarding its use. (This applied equally to all, to pupils as well as Heads). Finally they were assured that every effort would be made to ensure their anonymity in any final account.

Sometimes our colleagues and pupils seemed to view our ethical procedures as nit-picking. In the case of pupils it seemed they felt we had an automatic right to demand information by virtue of our 'authority'. However we persevered in our nego-tiations because, in the case of pupils, we wanted them to see that we valued their right to privacy. In the case of colleagues, we realised that they did not always consider how what they said might be construed by others.

In reality, problems associated with the negotiation of access to, and control of, data often appeared minor compared with the sheer mechanical difficulties of collecting it. Finding time among a host of other commitments was undoubtedly the biggest problem. Recording one's own classroom was not too difficult if a tape recorder was used, but arranging interviews and chasing responses to questionnaires was more time-consuming. For a whole term, MJ devoted most of her break times and lunch hours to interviews with sixty-five pupils. On the other hand, DE was able to set aside time from the non-teaching parts of the day. For example he used registration time, form time, the odd assembly missed, duty time on a summer's day on the games field, and clearing up time at the end of lessons in the lab.

It was a constant source of surprise how co-operative pupils were. It was as if a trade-off had taken place, involving an exchange of quiet non-intrusive co-operation during this non-teaching time for the opportunity to have their views and perceptions seriously discussed. We were also surprised at the willingness with which pupils gave up their own free time to come and talk to us and indeed MJ found pupils whom she had not invited arriving to contribute along with those with whom she had made appointments. One boy, whom she had regarded as 'poorly motivated', checked the time of his interview with her four times.

From the point of view of time, staff interviews were again more difficult to arrange. DE resorted to meeting colleagues in a pub, standing the cost of drinks in exchange for an interview usually recorded in the car (which when stationary allows for recordings of almost studio quality). It was during this data gathering phase that we ironed out simple methodological and procedural details. We found that individual or small groups of children responded in a more relaxed, less distanced manner if we provided coffee; that better recordings were obtained in a small, carpeted room, such as a careers' room, than in a more sparse tutor room.

It is often hard to pick out and reflect upon what is significant and what is merely 'noise'. One of the problems is learning how to reappraise what has been thought of as merely institutional 'noise' and hear it with 'new ears'. In a school with a public address system, DE had become so inured to its disembodied commanding edicts, that its messages went unremarked. Until, that is, the realisation dawned that the electronic voice carried illuminating evidence with respect to hidden curriculum. In the same school he had also accepted differential treatment of boys and girls unquestioningly; but the implications of this, that large parts of the school were in fact 'no go' areas for one sex or the other, was not appreciated. Even the assembly hall had a male half and a female half, a feature that was obvious, but which had actually gone un-noticed for ten years.

Perhaps because the collection of material had been so time-consuming we tended to postpone analysis. Eventually we wondered whether we were not avoiding the analytical task by imagining that we needed to collect yet more data; it took a considerable effort of will to make us move forward. However, we began to realise that, whilst we had not written much down, we had, in the natural course of events started to interpret our data by identifying issues and dimensions and postulating rela-tionships. All we really needed to do was describe these more explicitly, and systematically search our data for evidence that would confirm or refute our working hypotheses. We would certainly advise other teacher-researchers to consider processing their research as it progresses, and not to regard it necessarily as a subsequent activity. We also think it is important to stress that analysis begins in something we all do quite naturally, i.e. interpret events, because initially we felt quite daunted by the task for which we believed we lacked both experience and expertise.

Initially we used a simple list of main issues for a first crude selection of evidence. Most of our data was on cassette tapes and we needed to select potentially relevant passages before trans-cribing them for more detailed analysis. This task we had to do for ourselves in long hand. We calculated that it took approximately five hours to transcribe just half an hour of taped interview. (Classroom interaction took longer still.) Although costly in time we did find this exercise fascinating. When an idea starts to gel and evidence piles up to amplify it, the satisfaction is deep. When a cherished idea is no longer tenable in the light of evidence, an odd feeling of satisfaction remains, for one knows then that the research enterprise is justified and necessary.

As a second stage, MJ found it helpful to annotate data according to the categories or dimensions which had emerged. Using a card index these could then be cross-referenced and work could begin on looking carefully for patterns and relationships. Finally we developed a number of operational hypotheses that we believed are open to testing by others in other schools. For example, these were among the thirty-one hypotheses that MJ eventually derived:

> Teachers and parents who are familiar with Social Science see the function of Social Studies as the development of analytical skills, whereas these who know little of Social Science believe it to be 'training for life'.

> Pupils either perceive Social Studies to be based on common-sense knowledge and, therefore, 'easy', or based on expert knowledge and therefore 'hard'.

Among DE's twenty-eight hypotheses were these:

> If teachers play down individual differences among pupils (as in mixed ability groups), then pupils will play up basic gender differences.

> When pupils see boy–girl differences to be important, the girls find science acceptable only when it involves a functional, attractive, decorative product.

Of course, this stage of research will appear differently according to the kind of research questions asked and the methods chosen to elicit answers.

MJ was greatly helped at this time by being able to exchange a teaching commitment with a colleague and so freeing one whole afternoon a week. This was safeguarded by a deputy head who guaranteed her regular time to work on her analysis. Without some such arrangement it is difficult to imagine how teachers could accomplish anything substantial. For DE, having left the school, time was made available in his new employment.

Two other issues caused us some concern at this stage. First we were uncertain about the validity of our findings. This problem seemed particularly acute because we were working in our schools largely on our own, and it was perhaps exacerbated by the expectations of colleagues, for instance, for DE as a biologist to produce a statistical study. Both of us felt it important to find some critical friend, either inside or outside the school, and preferably one of each, who would be prepared, at least, to read our analysis and discuss with us its credibility in the light of the evidence we had collected. Ideally, of course, we would have liked them to check all our findings against our data but we had to admit that their lack of time made this largely impracticable.

MJ was concerned over the extent to which acknowledgement of existing theory should be made in any analysis. Eventually she decided to refer to theory when it illuminated further her own analysis; to this end Nell Keddie's work[2] was helpful when describing teachers' and pupils' perceptions of a specialist subject area. In our view little is to be gained by forcing teacher research into a particular theoretical framework. However, to ignore existing theory deliberately might be equally short-sighted.

There comes a point in any research when, despite the burgeoning of new and interesting issues for enquiry, the researcher has to decide that 'enough is enough', and apply himself to writing, then releasing his report. Despite the feeling of incompleteness one can always look to a new day to do what remains. When we were experimenting with our pieces of research it took a long time for us to register this simple truth and take the batteries out of our tape recorders and close our card indexes. Secretly perhaps we were striving to produce the definitive work on the whole educational system.

Eventually, examination deadlines loomed and had the effect of concentrating our minds remarkably. However, a few further issues had to be dealt with before we could finally put pen to paper. First we had to decide who we were reporting to. At the beginning of our research we did not see the implications of multiple audiences. Were we reporting to ourselves or our colleagues in our schools? Did our potential audience include 'outsiders', and if so, who were they? Our work was to be assessed by 'academics', but we were also interested in what it could tell us and our colleagues about our local situations. Insofar as our experience might correspond with that of other teachers elsewhere we were also interested in communicating with other teacher groups.

With these multiple audiences now in mind we next had to decide on an appropriate mode of reporting. MJ resolved this problem, by writing several reports, with different styles and emphases. One was a long and fully substantiated report[3] which was submitted both to the examiners and to the school. However, realising that few teaching colleagues (or pupils) would have the time or inclination to wade through 192 pages of typescript, a condensed version was written, for the school. This had the character of an evaluation and drew out the practical implications of the research. Subsequently a few themes that she imagined might be of interest to those who shared her subject specialism were extended and submitted in the form of an article to a relevant journal, the *Social Science Teacher*. In a sense this chapter represents a report to a fourth audience. DE's accounts of his research were responses to similar events and situations.[4,5]

Our research was conducted in our own schools and classrooms where we had some, if restricted, power to influence change. Thus we could not easily ignore the practical implications and we were forced to reconsider our researcher role. One question concerned whether we should present non-judgmental reports, or whether we should assume some responsibility for action by offering evaluative comments or suggestions regarding future practice. In reality we found it difficult to be non-judgmental. Apart from the impossibility of total objectivity we found people wanting us to express the opinions we had developed as a result of our research. In other words, they wanted to know what difference it made to us in order to assess the difference it might make to them. At least, this was the thrust of one Head's interest.

To suggest, however, that the impact of our research was either widespread or deep would be misleading. Whilst it absorbed us for some considerable time, our colleagues regarded it as no more than a peripheral activity of marginal interest. A few teachers were genuinely interested and responded constructively, but we tend to think that this had more to do with the quality of our relationships with them than the quality of our research effort. In the end we had little evidence of whether it made any real difference.

If this last observation seems unduly pessimistic and inappropriate to end on, then we would respond that it takes more than two small pieces of research to change two schools.

Nevertheless, if we had extended our own professional skills a little and suggested a few possibilities to a few others in passing, then, for the moment, we were content and could look forward to the next small step. We believe that for the most part professional development proceeds by small increments through engaging on research. For example, we think we reached a better appreciation of, and respect for, the individuality of our pupils. Whereas, formerly, we had assessed only those abilities that we defined as desirable, we were now made aware of these qualities of a human life that are often undervalued or ignored when the process of schooling takes on a narrow focus. In other words, we found the activity of research to be both educative and humanising.

REFERENCES

1. Becker, H. S., *Sociological Work: Method and Substance*, Aldine Publishing Co., Chicago, 1970.
2. Keddie, N., 'Classroom knowledge', in Young, M. F. D. (ed.), *Knowledge and Control*, Collier-Macmillan, London, 1971.
3. James, M. E., *Talking about Life: a study of teaching and learning sociology and social studies*, Unpublished M.A. Dissertation: University of London, Institute of Education, 1979.
4. Ebbutt, D. P., *Girls' Science; Sex Roles and the Curriculum*, Unpub-

lished M.A. Dissertation: University of London, Institute of Education, 1979.
5. Ebbutt, D. P., 'Girls' science: boys' science revisited' in Kelly, A. (ed.), *The Missing Half: Girls and Science Education*, Manchester University Press, 1981.

ALAN ROOT

Working with a colleague

In June 1979 I was coming to the end of a part-time education course which had been classroom based and asked me to look very closely at my teaching. Although I was going back to full-time teaching and was not going to have the support of a college or a tutor, the process was one that I did not want to give up. I wanted to find a research method that would help me to continue evaluating my own teaching. I knew, however, that it would have to be a method which could be operated with a limited number of resources and within the normal demands of the school day.

When I started to ask around about teacher operated evaluation a tutor mentioned the Ford Teaching Project (see Appendix). I started to read the materials that were available and felt that they were just right and I broadly followed their techniques in my research. At the same time a friend who was also involved in some action research in a neighbouring school asked if I would like to visit some of his lessons as an observer; as I was teaching part-time I could fit it into the time being offered. The opportunity of working with someone who had experience in action research was a key factor affecting my decision to carry out the research in another school. Also the teacher's subject, drama, was my own specialism; one which is not liberally spread around most timetables and therefore does not provide so many opportunities for collaborative work. There was also the added attraction of breaking new ground away from base camp.

On my first visit, I simply sat in on the class that was going to be involved. It was a mixed ability class (lasting eighty minutes) of some twenty-five 13 year olds in a co-educational comprehensive. I did not know what I was looking for, what to write down, or whether writing was the best form of recording. By the end of the lesson I had a collection of rambling notes that were very hard to make sense of. When the students had gone the teacher and I sat down and talked about the class and how we thought we could work together. Neither of us wanted then to discuss the other's check lists or observation techniques. We just wanted to get used to being in the same classroom together.

In the second observation lesson, I used a watch and a simpler version of the scheme described in the next chapter: in two-minute sections I simply noted what I felt to be the most dominant or, to me, important contribution to the lesson and from whom it came. At the end of this lesson I asked if I could talk to a group of the students. There were six of them in this group and we talked about the lesson for about twenty minutes (the duration of break). I asked them what they thought about the lesson and what happened in the classroom. I asked them to describe the lesson chronologically, saying what they thought was the most important point within each section. I emphasised that although I was taking notes, everything discussed was confidential, and asked many times if there was any part of our conversation which they would like to keep private. After this interview I talked to the teacher, in his free time that morning, and asked him to go through the same process, writing up a narrative of the lesson.

My own concerns, I decided, could wait. The teacher must first feel at ease with the process. The method evolved over the term, until the week's sequence looked like this:

1. The observer makes notes of the lesson in progress.
2. In the last ten to fifteen minutes of the lesson two or three groups of about three or four pupils are given tape recorders and go through the questionnaire, sometimes by themselves or perhaps with the observer as interviewer. Each week a new group is trained to use the questionnaire and tape recorder, until the whole class is involved.

At the end of the lesson, immediately
3. the teacher, with a tape recorder, goes through the questionnaire during break,

while
4. the observer writes up notes on the lesson using the questionnaire as a guide and referring to the notes made in section 1.

At a later time (two days later, in this case) the observer
5. transcribes the tapes;
6. types up all accounts, numbers all statement lines and puts these transcripts in display form;
7. goes through the transcripts noting agreement and disagreement.

Later on
8. the observer presents the display of the transcripts and also the notes to the teacher and these are debated.

Again later (in our case just before the next lesson)
9. transcript display and issues are presented to teacher and students for debate. The observer takes over as chairperson.

From my field notes I also include a short breakdown of the time I needed to carry out the research. When I first wrote it, I intended it to be for discussion, to make clear the time that teachers would have to demand if they were going to implement a similar programme inside the structure of a school. As the observer I found that the method which evolved became relatively easy to operate.

The first four stages listed below took the lesson time, of course, plus approximately fifteen minutes at the end of the lesson (which happened to fit very conveniently into the timetable). Stages five to seven varied in length, but each transcript took approximately thirty minutes; the analysis of the transcripts could take a further thirty minutes, although an interesting one could take an hour or so. Stage eight needed to be at least an hour long, and stage nine at least half an hour.

Stages	Section	Time	
		Hrs	Mins
1 and 2	Lesson	(1	20)
3 and 4	Teacher and Observer separately		15
5	Transcribe teacher tape		30
	Transcribe Group 1 tape		30
	Transcribe Group 2 tape		30
	Transcribe Group 3 tape		30
6	Typing	(approx 2 hrs)	
7	Noting issues (average)		45
8	Interim meeting with teacher	1	00
9	Teacher, students, observer		30
		4	30

Thus the total time needed was a minimum of 4 hours 30 minutes, plus the time of the lesson, and whatever time it took me for typing and collating. In 'real time' it tended to work out at most of a morning for stages 1–4; an afternoon for stage 5; an evening for stage 6; another evening for 7 and 8; and another lesson for stage 9 (in this case, registration period).

Several weeks after the completion of the experimental term, I made some general notes on the method we have employed. What follows is an edited version of those field notes using the stages described above.

At stage one I was an observer, making field notes during the lesson. I wrote down the lesson plan as it unfolded, noting key contributions by the teacher or the students within each phase. I also used a time sequence during the long phases. This process became easier and more enjoyable as the research went on. I never became part of the lesson for this seemed to fit into the pattern of these lessons. I thought at times that it would be possible to observe and participate, but this would have confused the role of the observer who would have become both a positive contributor and a passive follower.

In stage two the interviews with the students at the end of the lesson were at first with a group of five volunteers. We talked about the lesson, and I taped our conversation. Together with the teacher's notes made just after the lesson, this gave me a record of the lesson from three perspectives. I read this several times. The level of agreement between the comments was notable. At certain points in the lesson, however, there were strong disagreements between the contributors. I went through the same process for the third lesson. The teacher and I felt it was now time to have a detailed discussion about this piece of research. The ensuing meeting was an important point in the research. I wanted to talk about the documentation which I had typed up; the teacher was much more concerned with the organisation, the practical problems of writing up the lessons within the limited time of a school week. Although our aims conflicted, we agreed to streamline the interviewing by using a list of questions to provide a framework for the discussions. We both agreed on an outline of research and a timetable for carrying it out. We eventually gave each small group of about five students a casette tape recorder and the following guidelines:

Talk Rules
1. Make sure each person has the chance to speak on each part.
2. Offer your own views, even if they are different from the others.
3. Listen to others and help them get their ideas clear.

What to Do
1. Make a simple plan of the lesson.
2. For each part of the lesson, discuss the following points (for each section):
   a) What did you do?
   b) What did the class do?
   c) What were you asked or told to do?
   d) What did you do on your own initiative?
   e) Which were the good bits? – Why?
   f) Which were the not so good bits? – Why?
   g) Which were the hard bits? Explain.
   h) Who was the most important character to the drama and why?

Summing Up
1. How did this lesson link with past drama lessons?
2. How could this link into future lessons?

This framework was formulated from the issue which seemed to crop up in the interviews during the first three lessons. The questions were framed with the agreement of the teacher and reflected some of the issues which dominated the drama teaching. They may seem to be leading questions, but nevertheless they had the desired effect. The phrases had been negotiated with the students, who had developed a private language from previous interviews. It was clear in our minds that the list was designed for this class for this subject, and was not an attempt to cover any other situation.

Next I introduced the questionnaire-guide explaining that it would be helpful if they, the students, could conduct their own interviews with the tape recorders in my absence. In the next week group one were running their own interview and I took another group of students and went through the same process with them. By the sixth lesson there were three groups operating their own interviews. At this stage the replies were becoming superficial and so I felt the need to re-enter some of the groups as interviewer to encourage the students to expand upon their comments.

Stage three was during the morning break at the end of the lesson. The teacher, alone with a tape recorder, went through the same questionnaire-guide that the students had used, as did the observer. This stage evolved as the research went on. After the first lesson the observer and the teacher simply talked over the lesson together making brief notes that the teacher would write up afterwards. After the second and certainly in the third lesson this informal feedback was obviously not working and the first 'contract of expectations' was drawn up at the meeting with the teacher. This sounds very formal, but it seemed that something of this sort was essential. It was only when we had such an agreement that certain stages in the content of the work were clarified. In retrospect I believe we should have had a similar 'contract of expectations' with the students.

During stage four the observer, also alone, went through the questionnaire referring to the field notes from stage one. The stage one notes were shorthand remainders of my thoughts during observation and it seemed important to record them in full before they disappeared or were modified by time or the comments of others. This is why the students' self-interview was attempted, but, as previously stated, I had to sacrifice this detachment. Therefore towards the end of the term I tried to compensate by making my stage one notes more comprehensive.

Stage five always took place later on in the week when I transcribed my own tape and those from the student groups and the teacher. This meant that I locked myself away with a tape recorder and a pair of headphones and in long hand wrote down virtually word for word the contents of the tapes.

In stage six I typed my long hand transcripts and constructed a display of them. I taped together five sheets of foolscap, side to side. On the left was the teacher's transcript, then those of the three groups were next, and on the right was the observer's. Since everyone followed the same questions, it was possible to arrange the typing so that the answers to each question could be read across from left to right, starting with the teacher's and ending with the observer's. If more paper was required, then an extra sheet could be fixed underneath the first one. Though it took up a lot of space, it was invaluable for analysis. It was the only real way of cross-referencing the transcripts.

Stage seven was the noting of agreements and disagreements from the transcript display; for example, in one set of transcripts the teacher said,

> 'the large group work seemed out of place . . . I think my role stifled the kids' initiative . . .'. One of the students stated about the same phase,
> 'a not so good bit was doing the large play . . . when sir told us what to do; I would rather do something myself.'

In another set of transcripts a seeming disagreement emerged; the teacher stated,

> 'I was structuring, articulating the next move . . .';

the observer stated,

> 'The teacher held it together . . .';

and a student stated,

> 'The teacher did not tell us anything, really.'

I would look for agreement/disagreement cross references and put them into general issues. Having done that, I would read the rest of the transcript to see if any other themes arose. While an issue would occasionally be raised by an isolated comment most had at least two or three supporting statements. There was never any need to search for issues. Several were always obvious from the transcripts.

Stage eight was a meeting between the teacher and myself to discuss the transcript display and my cross-referencing. I would take the teacher through the transcripts and my comments; we found plenty to discuss. I would then leave a copy of the transcripts with the teacher. Because of lack of time I never got a copy of the transcripts to the teacher before this meeting. It would have been an advantage had I managed to do so.

The next stage (nine) was a meeting with the students together with the teacher and observer; it took the same format as stage eight, only this time the students were part of the debate. The only time we had available for this was a fifteen minute slot after morning registration and before the actual lesson started. This was far too short, and we rarely achieved anything of real value with the students in these circumstances. It was the most disappointing stage of all. None of us came to terms with it. Some of the reasons for this could have been: the lack of common goals with the students; the lack of involvement of the students; their lack of real power to affect the method that was offered; or, perhaps, we were working in the wrong mode. Interesting work could be done here; it was at this stage I really felt the disadvantages of being a visitor to the school. Perhaps this stage should have fitted into the students' chosen pattern instead of being squeezed into the registration period just before the lesson; it should have been as informal as my discussion with the teacher.

I have limited this chapter so far to the practical implementation of this piece of research, and though it was difficult not to refer to the content of the work, I have cut out nearly all documentation. However I should like to consider now some key points, taking them chronologically, which concerned us about our method during this particular piece of work.

First, from the observer's point of view: one of the major steps in organising the research was the meeting with the teacher after the third lesson. It was at that meeting that the research really started and there were several decisions made at that time which I think are important for the beginning of such a project. The timetable was an important factor for me. It seems essential that all contributors make clear the amount of time and effort that they can give, and agree upon a timetable for the completion of each stage. Certainly, for myself, if the timetable had not been there, many of the transcripts or comments I prepared would not have been ready on time. The timing of this meeting seemed to be right, because I doubt if the commitment could have been made at the beginning of the first lesson. It needed the first few lessons for the difficulties and the hopes of the work to become clear, so that a realistic commitment could be made. At the crucial meeting the teacher stated that the serious intention of those involved must also become clear; that a piece of research can so easily become a game, and that one must enter knowing that there is a duty to perceive oneself, one's collaborators and the classroom more clearly, and thereby improve the teaching.

For the teacher, an issue in the early stages was the confidentiality of the tapes and the transcripts. Certainly this was a point that I stressed with the pupils, but at no time did it become a problem in our project. The observer in our method had the editorial power over the tapes, and as the issues of confidentiality did not pose any problems or restrictions, the tapes were transcribed in total.

Once the research was under way, then, as observer, my continuing concern was with the interviewing. The questionnaire was produced to make the task of interviewing the teacher and the students easier. In our study it was only possible to obtain the students' comments directly after the lesson. I chose to gather exclusively oral data as being easier to obtain within the time limits, and to analyse, than either written (discursive or creative) or drawn responses. This was why tape recorders were used with the groups.

To begin with, I interviewed the students after the lessons and then interviewed the teacher. When this was done I would attempt to write up the observer's account. The problem was that by now I had shared the perceptions of the other contributors and could not decide if my comments were affected by those interviews. A possible solution to the problem was to write up the observer's account before the interviews; in the time available this was impossible. Neither teacher nor students could wait while I wrote up my account. The solution was to have a guideline for the contributors to conduct their own interview. An additional benefit of the questionnaire for the compiler of the transcripts was that it made the cross-referencing easier because the comments were organised under these general headings. Did the questionnaire guide too much, or even distort the responses of the teacher or the students? The real answer is that I do not know; all I do know is that the self-conducted interviews resulted in comments that, when linked with those of the observer, illuminated the classroom. The teacher seemed able to express all he wanted to through the guidelines, and the students seemed to be able to express some of their perceptions of their lesson too. But still I wanted more. The self-interviews were throwing light on issues in the classroom, but I wanted some of the comments to be elaborated. So, towards the end, I sacrificed the role of observer in order to adopt that of interviewer again with some of the groups. This time I found the interviewing exciting. At the beginning of the research I could not get to grips with the direction of the interviews. Now, with the questionnaire as the guide, all I had to do was just encourage the elaboration of the one sentence answers from the students. It was in these interviews that I felt most at ease, in a discussion about the lesson, not in a question and answer exercise.

The mode of reflection was an issue which concerned me. The questionnaire seemed to encourage a particular form of reflection, that of discussion in a detached, analytical way. This disturbed me all through the research, for two reasons: the students were becoming used to analysing the lessons in this way; and we limited ourselves to this one form of reflection. The question of whether the students can reflect in this way is crucial. Were we asking the students to use a mode of reflection in which they were too inexperienced, or was it that they were too immature? It is a very simple conclusion to draw. Many students found it difficult to express ideas and they did not seem to get to grips with the questions; the conclusion was that at that stage these students were not able to reflect in this way. I think our conclusion was right, for the simple reason that this type of reflection was not normally encouraged in the school, or at least that this type of reflection was not encouraged about the students' classrooms or the content of their lessons. I think we were asking the students to do something that was unusual in a school. We were asking them to have their own opinions about the classroom. It is a big step to take, and is not as simple as having an opinion on the content of that which the teacher presents to you. I think we asked a lot from the students at the start, and that towards the end of the research they were beginning to make a valuable contribution.

I found this issue of the varying modes of reflection difficult but interesting. In this research we took most of the time getting used to operating the method of collecting reflection through talk. Other modes, although talked about, were not used. I could speculate on the use of different ways of reflection, but speculation is all it would be. The investigation of different modes of reflection will certainly be the next step I will take in developing this method of research.

Another important process was the transcription. There were times when I wanted to pack up the lot and send it to an audio-typist; but I think that the transcribing was an important factor in my becoming fluent with the data. It certainly helped me when analysing the lesson either with the transcript display in front of me, or when just generally talking about the research. Perhaps this stage should not have been denied to the other contributors. The control of and familiarity with the data was very helpful in analysis and debate about the transcripts.

The time spent evolving the method and involving the students was the major issue for the observer at the end of the research. Such projects must be able to be conducted by teachers who have normal teaching loads. This is central to the research method. The practical problem is that the system encourages those involved to experiment with the process and to solve the problems that their particular situation poses. This means that a great deal of time is spent in developing the method. One of the principles of this work, however, was that the experimenting with perceptions is an essential part of the research process. Methodological considerations were central to what we were learning about the classroom.

There is evidence that throughout this research both the teacher and I committed one of the deadly sins of education. For it was we who learned most at the expense of the students. Dorothy Heathcote, a specialist in educational drama, once commented at a conference that 'the teacher . . . gets his or her mind sorted out at the expense of the kids'. That is exactly what the teacher and the observer were doing in this piece of research. One of us actually said at one point: 'when we get the method right that is the time to include the students'. By so doing we effectively excluded them from one of the most important phases, that of evolving a way of doing research.

I think this is crucial, for all the way through we were saying to ourselves that we must share power and what we were in fact doing was denying them any share whatsoever. It is such an easy trap to fall into that I feel it is important to state that it is impossible to do the research *without* the students; it is impossible to do the research *for* the students; only those involved can do it *with* the students. My interest now lies in developing a research method which does include the students.

JOHN SMIDDY

Creating a team

Hackney Downs School is a boys' comprehensive school of about 950 pupils. Formerly a grammar school, it became a comprehensive in 1968. Hackney is one of the poorest boroughs in London and its multi-ethnic nature became reflected in the composition of the school. The intake now had a full range of ability and many of the pupils or their parents came from the New Commonwealth, mainly the Caribbean. The staff tried to react positively to the school's new status. The changes it had undergone acted as a spur to the consideration of curriculum and teaching methods.

Part of this response was the development of the humanities department in the second half of the 1970s. The humanities department covers English, drama, history, geography and social studies, and an integrated curriculum was developed which had been extended from the first to the third year by 1979. The department planned its development carefully and without haste. It holds regular fortnightly meetings and has a residential weekend conference every year (there are twenty-seven full- and part-time teachers in the department). Integration is seen in terms not only of subject content, but also in giving consideration to subject skills and conceptual and language development. Teaching methods are understood as the means of transmitting knowledge, skills and concepts, and also as a means of developing pupils' imaginative, social and emotional selves. The department is committed to multi-cultural education, not only through the content of the humanities course, but also by trying to engender respect and understanding of other cultures.

The complexity of the task and the teachers' commitment made us recognise that constant self-education and sharing of expertise and experience was essential for progress. Teachers prepare and give papers and share lesson plans in department meetings, and are frank about both their successes and their failures in the classroom. At department meetings staff will describe the lessons they have taught and try to explain why they have or have not worked. This process of sharing enables us to attempt to bridge that gap between theory and practice. Often books on education by academics, although interesting and stimulating, are difficult to apply to classroom practice. The individual teachers are so overwhelmed by the daily practicalities that they have no time to think rationally about their pedagogy. Only too often talk between teachers is on the level of oaths on the bloody-mindedness of 3X, or the latest exploits of A, that notorious pupil in the second form.

Each humanities class is a mixed ability form taught by a team of teachers, consisting of an English specialist, a drama teacher and one history, geography or social studies specialist. Remedial reinforcement is given within the classroom by a specialist remedial teacher, usually for three periods a week. A class has eight or nine periods of humanities a week; typically, third year classes would have eight periods a week. In two of these lessons the class has drama, taken by the drama specialist and another teacher. The rest of the lessons are divided between an English teacher and a subject specialist teacher, who are timetabled to teach together for two of those lessons.

The class team of teachers plan their lessons together and prepare the necessary materials. The team prevents the isolation felt by many secondary school teachers, and provides a supportive group for examining the success of lessons. The department is well resourced with books, film strips and video cassettes, and work sheet masters, as well as a wide range of information sources. It is also ably supported by a media resources department, and the school office readily does any required typing.

Hackney Downs School, like most others, does not make allowances on the timetable for teachers to act as classroom observers for others. It was only by luck that I was able to undertake this for one double period a week, when a timetabled CEE course failed to attract sufficient numbers. The head of humanities and I came up with this solution as a way of using these periods more constructively than merely doing cover periods, and the headmaster and his deputy – who is in charge of the timetable and its daily operation – agreed to it. The teacher whose class I wished to observe had previously agreed to me coming into his lesson.

There were limitations on my choice of class. First, the teacher of the class had to be sympathetic to, and agree to, my observation. Secondly, the class had to fall in the double period I had available on a Thursday morning before break. Finally, I wanted to observe a relatively experienced humanities teacher's class, because I felt that such a teacher would be more at ease with an observer and would better represent the sort of work that was going on in the department. The class I observed was a second form which, in this double period, was being taught by an English teacher, reinforced by another English teacher acting as a remedial help.

The main reason I started the research was that I felt a more detailed and methodical observation of the classroom would inform and raise the level of discussion at department meetings. If this experiment proved useful I hoped that classroom research could be used more widely in the department. I also felt that, if I decided on too narrow a focus before starting the research, its impact might well be limited. The issues, I hoped, would emerge from the observation itself. As I wanted to engage the interest and co-operation of the class teachers, I was anxious to involve them as fully as possible in defining the main areas of concern.

I used two main methods of observation. First, I made field notes when sitting at the back of the class. (It seemed to me initially that field notes were simple to make, requiring no extra equipment, and would enable me to get a general overview of the class and its activities. From this general view I hoped a focus would emerge which could require a different method of observation. The following are the first notes taken from a longer sequence.)

1. Sitting in traditional rows. Four rows of five desks.
2. He settles class as folders and texts given out by pupils.

3. Pupils give out folders and texts. H gives out worksheets.
4. R stands at front not participating in activity.

The numbers represent the sequence of events rather than the minutes of the lesson. This method had limitations; you could not hear and record conversations between teachers and individuals and groups of pupils and between pupils themselves. I used this method for the first lesson only. These limitations forced me to record teacher initiatives and pupil responses and general classroom organisation. I therefore decided to use a tape recorder to record the activities of one group of pupils and any whole-class teacher-led discussions. The group I generally chose to record was a lively one, in which the two teachers who normally taught the class were particularly interested, as part of their concern with language development. (Both teachers were studying language development in a group organised by the London University Institute of Education.) The use of a tape recorder helped to create the first real focus because it narrowed the number of pupils being studied in detail.

I felt it was important that, after each period of research, the observations should be typed up and presented to the teachers for discussion. The teachers themselves wrote down after the lesson what their lesson aims were and how successful they thought the lesson had been. Once the recording was made, I listened to the whole tape and decided which bits to transcribe. I aimed to transcribe a representative sample of about ten minutes: usually the teacher instructing or discussing with the class or group, and a lengthy portion of group talk. This process took quite a few hours and I wrote it out in long hand. I then gave the transcriptions to the school office for typing, together with the teachers' comments on their aims and success. The lesson was on a Thursday morning, and the final documents were presented to the teachers early the next week. The following is an example of the class teacher's comments:

AIMS: *Following on from the work on Anglo-Saxon life*
1. To teach: structuring of A/S society. Numbers/power
2. To teach: a) start to look at the importance of asking certain questions about culture

b) how to find information from a book without being specifically directed to chapter and pages

c) to rearrange information in a book for new needs i.e. (2a)

3. To teach: how to present information in diagram form
4. To teach: concept of power – relative groups e.g. Anglo-Saxons

The reinforcing teacher made these comments on the same lesson:

It looked to me like a fairly successful lesson. The main activity proposed – the compiling of information from a mixture of textbook, teacher statements and suggestions, and learners' previous knowledge – may have been too hard for up to half the kids, but whether they achieved a finished end-product or not, nearly all seemed engaged in actually trying to crack the problem, and that was a good thing. They had this relatively easy task of designing a pyramid diagram to give them some sense of achievement on the page. It was excellent that almost no straight copying occurred throughout the double lesson. I suspect that's a rarity for any lesson that involves an amount of factual input . . .

J and I (particularly I) should have been more certain about several key pieces of information, e.g. were there more churls than thralls?

A useful idea might be to repeat an exercise involving the compilation of information from various sources, but with a bit more exact knowledge on our part about where the information can be found. I don't mean spoonfeeding at all; perhaps narrowing down the field so that the kids have four or five pages to scan rather than a whole chapter . . .

I wasn't quite sure that the extra labour involved in producing two worksheets rather than one was worthwhile, when the questions on each were substantially the same. Would the second worksheet and the main questions written on the board have been enough?

I think a central problem with worksheets/questions/bits of information is that they tend to produce *bits* of writing. Little three or four line splodges. Could we think about a way of getting the kids to write more fluidly, more discursively, and at somewhat greater length and consecutiveness?

(In the same lesson, I noted that a good proportion of the class lacked enthusiasm for the tasks the teachers had set. A number seemed to require a great deal of help to do the tasks, and even with two teachers there was not enough individual help available. The teachers recognised this and the class teacher stopped the class a number of times to explain things.)

Arranging a time for us to discuss the lesson was very difficult because of the teaching and meeting commitments we all had, as well as administration, pastoral work, marking and preparation. Our meetings tended to be hurried because they were usually arranged for lunchtimes or in between lessons. We were able to arrange a morning of discussion in one school holiday. I tried not to force my ideas on the teachers but to ask open questions about the observations and explore the interests of the teachers with further questions.

Over the weeks our discussions increasingly became concerned with the pupils' language development and how lessons could be organised to extend the pupils' use of language and how informal pupil-to-pupil conversation differed from language use in formally organised classroom discussion exercises. The teachers were not only choosing to focus and use my observations in a particular way, but also I was increasingly choosing to record in detail the sort of material they were interested in. In this extract, the teacher had just stopped the class's written work. It is a good example of teacher-led discussion, showing many of the deficiencies typical in this kind of lesson. In later lessons the teachers tried to solve these problems by structuring the talk work differently.

H: Well let's not shout out. Let's just take it nice and steady. Mr Richmond will write the things up if you can just take it nice and steady. Shush. The question again. If life had been so hard for hundreds of years, why did the Vikings attack start to about 800? Why didn't they attack sooner? Now if you've got an idea then put your hand up and we'll try and get them down.

Pupil: . . . . .

H: What do you mean? Can you just put that in another way because I don't think we understood what you said.

Pupil: He means like that.

H: Go on.

Pupil: When the Vikings set off to Britain, that year it was very cold, sir, maybe they thought it was going to be like that all the time. (*Hubbub*)

H: Alright, just a second, Nigel, can you explain what he just said because I'm having difficulty understanding what he's getting at. Chris.

Chris: Sir, it's like it's colder than it's ever been, sir, like a year it might have been.

H: Where was it cold though?

Pupil: . . . . .

H: So, like we're saying. What time of the year?

Pupil: The winter.

H: So they might have had a very bad winter in Scandinavia and then at the end of that winter they said that well we can't stand another one like that, we better go.

R: Is that what you were saying or were you saying that they came to England one year, and it was an exceptional winter in England as well, like last winter. They thought blow this for a lark and went back. No.

H: Well, let's just make sure that everybody understands that. What he's saying is, the winter might have been so bad in Scandinavia that they were forced to look elsewhere for what?

Pupil: Land.

The teachers made very little use of the recordings to examine the effective learning of history or geography skills and instead concentrated on pupils' talk. This increasing focus is best illustrated by contrasting the teachers' earlier comments with the minutes of a later discussion where a recording of pupils' informal conversation from a lesson is discussed.

> The informal talk was talking for status. It was negative, about gaining an advantage and using opponents' mistakes. The talk was aggressive and combative and turned on the previous statement. Typical language of the school.

> This kind of talk illustrates well the point that the kids are skilful – interested in language skills and their development. In fact they are central to status and pleasure and entertainment.

> The skill lies in picking up the aggressive statement or implied insult or provocation and turning it against the opponent. They in fact listen to each other. They listen for their own purposes. There is immediate motivation for reply.

> The teacher is asking for something different than immediacy – long term understanding, to hold it. The teacher asks children to listen for a period of time without a context. Language is used for different purposes.

My role was one of a facilitator for the classroom teachers. I was providing the material on which the classroom teachers could focus and in discussions I became one of three people who were contributing to the analysis of that material.

Increasingly I became a participant observer in the class and it became impossible to be merely passive. The pupils, who are used to having more than one adult in the class, asked advice about their work, and the teacher often asked me questions of fact during the class discussions. The role of participant observer has definite advantages; it enables the classroom researcher to seem less threatening and more supportive to the others in-volved and it builds a team spirit and openness which might otherwise be difficult to develop. The pupils, because they are able to identify you as 'merely' another teacher, act more normally and therefore your observations are more valid.

In this case, the pupils in the class knew I was a teacher in the school, although I had never taught them. They had seen me around and I had, no doubt, taught some of their friends.

Because of this they treated me as a teacher, and in certain cases expected me to act as one and help them in their work. They also looked to me when they were up to some mischief, expecting me to react as a teacher, despite the fact that they had been told about the research. When working as a participant observer, the teachers, for their part, must not feel that you are prying, but they must feel involved in the research and able to influence its direction. If you are helping them in the class, relationships become easier, and more open.

The use of tape recording equipment caused all sorts of problems because we found it hard to get a good quality recording in a classroom. At first we used a simple cassette recorder with an internal microphone, but the Media Resources Officer in the school proved very helpful and arranged for us to use better equipment. Despite this, transcribing the recording proved to be very difficult and time consuming and the single forty-minute period that I had been allowed to use for this was inadequate, which meant that most of the work had to be done at home.

The classroom research had proved to be interesting and useful. It had increased the awareness of all the teachers and made us look at the classroom more rigorously and more critically. The main focus had developed into a careful examination of pupils' talk and we had found that certain types of lessons were more successful than others in stimulating useful pupil exploratory and analytical talk. We had not reached great new academic insights, but we had improved our own classroom practice. It is in the classroom where research has to be relevant if it is to affect our educational practice, and one way of improving that practice is by classroom teachers monitoring and analysing their own classrooms. For continuous progress and awareness to be maintained this had to be a regular process in a supportive atmosphere. Insights from this process can usefully be shared and difficulties of analysis can be collaboratively solved.

In order to stimulate the interest of the humanities department in classroom research I was to lead a session in the annual humanities weekend conference after the project had finished. I thought that in this context an activity-based session would be more rewarding than listening to another lecture and I had seen a simulation on an ILEA history course which gave me the idea to try a similar exercise. I organised a group of teachers to act as two small groups of pupils in a classroom and gave them a fifteen-minute lesson. The rest of the teachers recorded what was happening in four different ways.

The first group of teachers used one of the systems of observation I had seen used on the ILEA course (see Figure 1). Secondly, I asked some teachers to use the Flanders System of Interaction Analysis (Figure 2), but asked them to record an observation every thirty seconds rather than the normal three seconds for a trained observer. Other teachers I asked to make field notes on an individual pupil or on one of the groups. After the simulation the teachers were asked to form discussion groups containing people who had used the different forms of observation. The groups were asked to discuss the advantages and disadvantages of each method of observation, and if a system of classroom research had any place in the practice of the humanities department. The discussion in the groups brought up some interesting points. It was realised that the values of the observer became apparent in the language she/he used to describe the events. Others raised the point that their attention was caught by the noisy pupils. Observers felt that their immediate focus was on the teacher and classroom organisation and that they ignored the detail of the pupils' activity. All the observers recognised the complexity of interaction and activity and felt that it was necessary to focus any study. Colleagues came to appreciate the value of classroom research and now see its importance to the development of the department.

Next year classroom research will continue in the department and we hope that this bears fruit. We are obviously novices in this process and we must gain more knowledge and experience of classroom research methods, both by reading and by learning through doing – in exactly the same way as we try to teach our pupils.

Classroom action research has many advantages which

Figure 1. Observation of specified activities of one student for each minute[1]

Select any student in the group and record his or her activities minute by minute on the grid below by putting a tick against the dominant activity for that minute. You can tick two or more activities if these are going on together.

Note: *administration* = getting out books, pens etc., fetching resources.
 not involved = chatting about non-relevant matters, disruptive activity, doodling etc.
 practical = drawing, cutting out etc.

Time (minutes)	1	2	3	4	5	6	7	8	9	10	11	12	13	14	15
administration															
waiting attention															
not involved															
listening															
observing															
practical															
discussion															
deliberating															
reading															
writing															

Figure 2. *The Flanders System of Categories for interaction analysis*[2]

Watch the teacher during the lesson, and every thirty seconds write down the category number of the interaction you have just observed. Record these numbers in sequence in the column provided.

The ten categories

Teacher Talk	Indirect influence	1. ACCEPTS FEELING: accepts and clarifies the feeling tone of the students in a non-threatening manner. Feelings may be positive or negative. Predicting and recalling feelings are included.	
		2. PRAISES OR ENCOURAGES: praises or encourages student action or behaviour. Jokes that release tension not at the expense of another individual, nodding head or saying 'uh huh?' or 'go on' are included.	
		3. ACCEPTS OR USES IDEAS OF STUDENTS: clarifying, building or developing ideas or suggestions by a student. As teacher, brings more of his own ideas into play, shift to category five.	
		4. ASKS QUESTIONS: asking a question about content or procedure with the intent that a student answer.	
	Direct influence	5. LECTURES: giving facts or opinions about content or procedure; expressing his own idea; asking rhetorical questions.	
		6. GIVES DIRECTIONS: directions, commands, or orders with which a student is expected to comply.	
		7. CRITICISES OR JUSTIFIES AUTHORITY: statements, intended to change student behaviour from non-acceptable to acceptable pattern; bawling someone out; stating why the teacher is doing what he is doing, extreme self-reference.	
Student talk		8. STUDENT TALK-RESPONSE: talk by students in response to teacher. Teacher initiates the contact or solicits student statement.	
		9. STUDENT TALK-INITIATION: talk by students, which they initiate. If 'calling on' student is only to indicate who may talk next, the observer must decide whether student wanted to talk. If he did, use this category.	
		10. SILENCE OR CONFUSION: pauses, short periods of silence, and periods of confusion in which communication cannot be understood by the observer.	

permeate the life of the school. The pupils enjoy being the object of interest and like to talk about the record of what they have done. There can be no doubt that the class discussed here became more enthusiastic about and more critical of their work. Classroom teachers involved came to a better understanding of the classroom. The issues that we had examined in one class stayed in our minds when we taught other classes. The department and school benefit by being formally told about the research and by the research being talked about and used as evidence in many different contexts, whether it be informally in the staffroom or in curriculum planning meetings.

REFERENCES

1. This is based on a grid in *The Effective Use of Reading*, ed. E. Lunzer & K. Gardner, Schools Council/Heinemann Educational, 1979.
2. Taken from Bennett, N. & McNamara, D., *Focus on Teaching*, Longman, 1979, p. 100. See also Amidon, E. J. & Flanders, N. A., *The Role of the Teacher in the Classroom*, Minneapolis Ma.: P. S. Amidon, 1963.

NIGEL RUMBLE

Whole school strategies

For a number of years I have been Head of Science at a large comprehensive school in the southern part of England. As I firmly believe that evaluation has a central role to play in effective curriculum development, it is not surprising that I have become interested in developing and implementing various evaluation techniques. In more recent years I have become particularly concerned with problems associated with the dissemination of such innovatory programmes across the whole curriculum.

  The school at which I teach has a fine record of curriculum development and dissemination involving both the adoption and adaptation of national projects, and the development, as far as is possible, of courses from first principles. Typical of many schools we can identify, within our organisation, areas of strengths and weaknesses, and periods in the past that could be regarded as rather traumatic.

  It was during such a period, in the early to middle seventies, that I developed my first interest in the evaluation of performance. At that time the school had grown rapidly, doubling its size in terms of its buildings, and numbers of pupils and staff. Heads of Department and Houses were faced with the problems of working with predominantly young and inexperienced staff, who themselves were teaching children from a developing overspill estate, in a school environment that was both rapidly and radically changing. Life for a Head of Department was rather difficult and a complete contrast to earlier times when departments were small, experienced and stable. To make matters worse we had been without our Headmaster for a year – just the right time for a full-scale HMI inspection. Although many of us were a little apprehensive, we looked forward to the visit as a constructive exercise that would enable us to move forward.

A team of seven HMIs duly arrived to spend one week talking to and observing both staff and pupils. A report was later submitted to the school and made available to all Heads of Department. Those individuals or groups that received praise naturally accepted the report, and proceeded to pat each other on the back. Many of the individuals or groups, however, that had received some criticism found it all too easy to disregard the report as inaccurate, unrealistic or based on unacceptable criteria. I became particularly interested in this last observation, which can, by and large, be accounted for in the following three ways:

1. Whenever judgments are made they are based on an interpretation often based on personal values.

   One particular example of this springs to mind when an unfortunate colleague was, unbeknown to themselves, descended upon during different times in the same lesson by two Inspectors. Each made a comment concerning the same aspect of this work which completely contradicted the other.

2. During their relatively short stay some of the HMIs were making interpretations which should have involved the understanding, or at least awareness, of the very complex interaction that took place within the school and between the school and its immediate community. Many of us felt that five months would have been a more realistic time in which to understand what was going on than the five days available; could their interpretation be valid?

3. The last of the problems on acceptance of the report, and arguably the major one, relates to the area of teacher threat. Many of us are reluctant to accept valid criticism, as to do so could result in attracting the unwelcome interest of colleagues. Any discrepancy between acceptable perform- ance and actual performance will often lead to anxiety. For a teacher to survive in a school environment and receive promotion he must perform well, or at least lead others to

think that he can perform well. Those of us with performance discrepancies – most of us if we are honest – make the
right noises and retreat to our heavily fortified classrooms
so that others cannot see the cracks in our own armour. If
anyone points at us, we react by fighting back with any
weapons we can find. During the inspection rumours and
questions spread through the staffroom: 'Which HMI had
only taught in Grammar Schools?' 'Which one had said that
he became an HMI because he himself was a poor teacher?'

These and many other questions and comments were probably not based on truth, but were developed or exaggerated by
those reacting defensively. It is my impression that such reactions led to a lack of confidence for many in the HMIs and their
report.

Although some of us were initially disappointed with the lack
of an immediate spin-off from the visit, it at least provided a
stimulus to consider more effective forms of evaluation. At a
Heads of Department meeting it was suggested that it would be
a useful exercise if we could gather together for an extended, and
interrupted, period of time the nucleus of the staff to discuss
relevant issues. A small committee was set up with the responsibility for liaising with all members of staff in an attempt to
arrange a programme. An extended weekend course at the
authority's residential centre was eventually attended by about a
quarter of our staff. The majority of the authority's advisory
staff also attended and many led discussion groups. We were
also fortunate in obtaining several outside speakers including
HMI Murry White. It was during such discussions that the first
tentative ideas for a school-based evaluation policy were formulated.

I am firmly convinced that evaluation should be school/
teacher based and initiated, for three reasons:

1. As teaching takes place in a continuously changing context,
   any adopted evaluation strategy, if it is to be realistic, must
   therefore be both flexible and continuously operated. No
   school or department will be able to claim the time of

external evaluators. Further, any advisory/inspectorate service would be of limited help for three basic reasons:

a) Like any external evaluator they would not be able to
devote sufficient time, particularly if such a service were
widely adopted.

b) The expertise of the advisory staff may not be com-
patible with the task at hand. Many authorities may not
have had the need or foresight to select and appoint staff for
such work.

c) Many outsiders find it difficult to be accepted into
schools. Such people often pose a threat, real or imagined,
in that they take a directive or judgmental stance or are
associated with an administration involved in career and
promotion decisions.

2. The teacher is an integral and individual part of any
learning situation; the interaction between them and individual pupils must be unique. One could argue, for this
reason, that the teacher is the only individual who could,
with some assistance, be capable of undertaking the evaluation.

3. So as to minimise anxiety personal teacher development
would best take place if individuals could be encouraged to
recognise their own areas of performance weakness, set
their own levels of success and evaluate their own performance in achieving such goals.

The school based model has its inherent limitations. If a
school draws exclusively on its own resources there is a danger
of parochialism and bias. Development is dependent upon
obtaining relevant feedback on both the teaching methods
employed and the effects of such methods which must therefore
be collected from as many perspectives as possible.

Following our weekend session I became convinced that the
key to personal development was getting staff to become aware
of and accept performance weaknesses on their own accord. As I
was unaware of any suitable evaluation technique designed
specifically for such classroom use, I adapted one frequently

used in industry. Late in 1975 members of the Science Department were introduced to this idea of a personal training plan, based on regular meetings between individual department members and myself. Involvement in the plan was optional providing that staff could answer one question: 'Are you a perfect teacher?' If they could answer yes, they were questioned no further and could opt out. No one did.

The idea of the interview session was to get staff to become aware of their own performance in terms of strengths and weaknesses. Having done this, a personal training plan was developed by the member of staff in co-operation with myself. Staff were asked to identify and develop their own criterion of success and to monitor their own progress, as would the Head of Department. The response was good, although initially at a trivial level: 'I tend to turn up to lessons two or three minutes late'; 'I do not test out practical experiments before lessons'.

Such statements could be made freely at a low anxiety level but above all they enabled staff to be reassured about the way information was handled in confidence. Admissions made to me were regarded as a sign of strength and were never divulged to any other source without the permission of that member of staff. Within six months, many staff were being very open and were making admissions of a complex nature. Although the prime task in any self evaluation technique is to get the potential participants to recognise and accept a need for change, which I had felt had been accomplished, I still found it increasingly difficult to help. The problem was two-fold:

A. There was a difficulty in distinguishing between the perceived symptom of a problem and the original cause of the problem.
B. Having identified the real cause, what can one do about it? The traditional remedy would be to try to find a course, but none seemed to be or could ever be relevant. Few seemed to meet the needs of individual teachers in their particular teaching environments.

Training should not be confined to the design and development of courses, but to the evaluation of real needs within the school, and the soliciting of constructive and active support for all staff participation. It is this preparatory groundwork which I consider to be one of the priorities in training. My main concern is not how to develop any particular course designed to fulfil any surmised or perceived need, but how to identify fundamental problems and get those problems accepted so that action can be taken. Would it be too cynical to suggest that training at either school or local level often stems from such statements as:

A. 'They're not doing it the way they're supposed to.'
B. 'They don't have the correct attitude to teaching.'
C. 'Staff absenteeism is too high.'
D. 'Our Science or Technical Staff aren't safety conscious.'

These statements are often followed by the profound diagnosis: 'We have a training problem', and the prescription: 'Send them on a course'.

The treatment provided is thus often in the form of a multitude of one hour, one day, weekend or one year courses in the form of lectures, workshops and conferences at which staff volunteer, volunteer under duress, or are directed. I am not arguing against the need for DES or LEA courses, as the need for them surely exists. What I am arguing against is the practice of not matching the real needs of teachers with the provisions made either at school level or by external courses. If such matching is not carefully carried out there will be an obvious danger of staff seeing in-service training as a waste of time. On many occasions we have used either DES or LEA courses, and have found them to be valuable. On other occasions, however, we have found the unique nature of some problems more effectively dealt with at school level, although this has not stopped us from bringing into the school external assistance in the form of LEA advisers.

The questions I like to ask before any training design stage are thus the following:

1. Have we identified the problem or merely a symptom?
2. Does the problem justify an active training programme?
3. What 'off the shelf' courses are available?

4. Can a school-based programme be more effective and, if so, what external help, if any, will we require?

The trouble with the kinds of statements listed previously, (A) to (D), is that what people identify as 'the problem' often is not the problem at all, but a symptom. The need or problem is an expression of the discrepancy that exists between the teacher's own perception of his teaching performance and his actual teaching performance. Many of these discrepancies can be eliminated. Training is a remedy used to achieve desired results. It implies a transferal of information to change someone's state of knowledge or ability to perform. Why, however, send all technical staff on 'safety in the workshop' courses, when most staff are already aware of required safety standards and precautions? Further instruction is not likely to produce the desired results, as we are looking at a symptom of a problem and not a description of the real problem itself. What is needed is further insight into a problem, so that all can identify the root cause and then deal with it.

In our science department interview sessions, staff were becoming aware of, and admitting to many of the symptoms, but not to the root causes. How could we, in a low threatening environment, enable staff to become aware of such deep-seated causes by themselves? In my experience the directive approach, 'you ought to do it this way', is of limited value. It seemed essential to take another step and not just leave it to the staff to come up with the real causes. I had to find a way of providing feedback and present it in such a way as to enable staff to recognise and accept the root causes. How often does the intention of a teacher differ from the actual performance? How often do organisations provide any facility for looking at themselves? How often do people return from courses exclaiming 'what a waste of time – we already do it', when they probably do not? Anxiety and threat aroused by the provision of feedback, however, tend to prevent rather than encourage self reflection by teachers.

How then could I resolve the dilemma between providing feedback and minimising threat? At the same time I wanted the department to work as a single group, so that we could share our experiences and powers of observation. If I was asking staff to be frank about their performance in front of colleagues, I was introducing yet another source of threat, as teachers find it difficult to expose their own classroom problems to their colleagues. It seemed to me that many staff would feel that, because of their position in the hierarchy, the Heads of Department would have far more to lose if they admitted to having problems. We were fortunate in having a television studio at school so I set about making a number of recordings showing myself at work. At the time I was concerned about our general ability as a department to deal effectively with mixed ability groups pursuing a Nuffield orientated course. For this reason I used such a group as the basis for the study. For the next six months regular meetings were held at which members of the department were asked to employ various techniques in analysing my lessons. To be able to see that Heads of Department had faults and admitted to such faults provided, in itself, a reassurance to others. Within a short period of time other members of staff became willing to record their own lessons for group discussion. Although my initial lesson recordings were made on video tape, we soon confined ourselves to just using the transcripts made from audio tape recordings. The use of video obviously had its advantages but it had many disadvantages, particularly in the influence it had on classes who were subjected to the obvious presence of lighting, microphones, cameras and camera operators.

We attempted to make this programme as public as possible. A booklet was printed which explained to other staff what we were attempting to do, and was to form the basis of a discussion with other Heads of Department. Its cover showed a Lord Kitchener figure, in cap and gown, pointing to the reader and asking 'Are you a Perfect Teacher?' Such publications fulfilled two functions:

1. To provide for its participants some recognition and thus provide a source of motivation.
2. To provide a stimulus for similar activity in other parts of the curriculum.

During our previous weekend residential session we had discussed at some length the suspected problem of pupil under-achievement in the school. We wanted to find out whether there was a problem, and if so what that nature of the problem was. An open invitation was extended to all staff who were interested to take part in a working party to identify the nature of the problem and to come up with suggestions on how to deal with it. About twenty staff from school became closely involved in this work, as did the LEA's Remedial Adviser, the Adviser with special responsibility for our school, and the authority's educational psychologist. The advisers were brought in at our request, as we felt that they had a lot to offer and would enable us to deal more effectively with any outside agencies, particularly our feeder schools. Standardised diagnostic tests were administered by our own English and Remedial Staff to pupils in our school as well as to pupils in our five feeder schools. In an attempt to obtain a greater understanding, and develop confidence in each other's work, we also arranged joint informal staff meetings between our own staff and those of the feeder schools. Later, during a two week period, we arranged for several of our staff to teach in some of the feeder schools for several days at a time. It became apparent that many of the pupils entering our school had definite problems with basic literacy and numeracy. It was also apparent that it was very difficult to detect and deal with such problems with the limited contact time available between any given pupil and teacher in a typical comprehensive school.

After much discussion we decided to extend the usual primary school policy into our own first year. Experienced teachers, as well as being tutors to groups of first years, were also to become their general subjects teachers for one third of the pupils' timetable. This time was made available from timetable space previously occupied by such subjects as Humanities and Science. By extending the pupil contact with a given teacher we have now greatly minimised the problem. The course and materials were initially developed by the first year teachers although during this period one of the team had developed an interest in Jerome Bruner's 'Man: A Course of Study'. After attending a course he soon interested other General Subjects teachers of the possibility of adopting MACOS and arrangements were made for the team members to visit another school who were operating the course.

The General Studies team had been selected because of their individual experience and specialism covering the spectrum of the curriculum, but having decided to adopt MACOS they immediately found themselves under pressure. In view of the fact that they worked in time previously allocated to some of the more traditional departments (although given quite freely), they felt that they had to justify their own existence, and demonstrate the worth of the course. This meant two things:

A. The team had to get familiar with the new course, and become aware of the new skills and attitudes that it required.

B. They had to develop a sophisticated evaluation programme which would be of obvious use to themselves, but could also be available for general circulation.

At this stage I was invited by the course team to help them disseminate the philosophy of MACOS and acquire the skills required of them as teachers playing such a new role. Many hours were spent in using the materials made available by the local Teachers' Centre, and in talking to staff from other schools who were involved in MACOS and to local advisers, and in adding our own extended discussion sessions at school.

In evaluating the worth of our proposed course, we agreed that we did not want to see MACOS reduced to the level of most other subjects in the curriculum, which seem to have gone too far down the path of assessing the end product by recall of content. Such evaluations are usually non-diagnostic since they provide very little information about the factors which influenced the learning or understanding. Those familiar with MACOS will be aware that its success is greatly dependent on the interactions that take place between pupils and between pupils and teachers. We should not only be concerned with what teachers intend pupils to learn, but also with those values and attitudes which are, without the teacher realising it, conveyed to the pupils by the teaching style.

I now had an ideal situation in which to introduce the idea of self evaluation. In the Science Department I had spent a considerable amount of time and energy in gradually introducing self evaluation to an initially unreceptive group of teachers. With the General Studies teachers we had a ready-made group who, because of their own adoption of a somewhat radical course, realised that they themselves were learners. The General Studies group was now receptive to change and constructive discussion. Teachers are generally more open to the various forms of innovation in a situation of low security; the more security one has the more one has to lose. Our MACOS team had found themselves in a situation where they knew little about the project, and of course, no one expected them to know anything. What is perhaps more important is that the course team knew that other staff realised they were learning. They could afford to admit their ignorance without anxiety.

I took advantage of this situation by organising a week-end course at which we could continue the discussion at leisure. It was my intention to lead the discussion from course content to evaluation and to demonstrate the merits of self evaluation. My original aim had been to hold this course in our own school, although I would have preferred more pleasant surroundings. However we were employed by a generous authority, sympathetic to school-based curriculum development, and so I contacted one of the LEA Advisers and negotiated the use of the authority's residential centre. This, incidentally, provided official recognition and approval for our work, thus giving it status and in so doing additional motivation for the course team. The course was attended by all members of the MACOS team, our own Headmaster, the LEA Adviser whom I had previously contacted and invited with the team's permission, myself and the Head of English who, we felt, had much to offer. Within hours our discussion moved to the problems of evaluation of the course objectives. I took care not to push ideas onto the team too quickly and spent some time in talking about the problems of designing tests to measure the achievement of the MACOS objectives. We moved on to discussing several of the observational techniques employed to aid evaluation and were greatly impressed by the evaluation materials developed for the Schools Council 'Science 5–13' course.

One of those on the course was a member of the Science Department who was naturally adept at discussing and evaluating transcripts of her own lessons. I had previously asked her to bring along some of her lesson tapes and transcripts. This young teacher soon proceeded to lead the group in employing, in particular, some of the Ford T (see Appendix) techniques in analysing her lessons. Other members, who at my request had also brought tapes, soon volunteered for similar treatment. In the first instance we were very careful not to make value judgments about such lessons, as this would only increase anxiety. Such judgments should be made, at least initially, by the teachers themselves after being presented with or collecting statements of observations.

The MACOS teachers are now generally self sufficient in the sense that they are confident enough and have acquired the skills to employ, without outside help, many of the evaluation techniques as an integral part of their working day. Some of the skills that they have developed are, in the context of our school, unique to the team and a valuable source of expertise for other individuals or departments. Perhaps of greater significance is the influence these teachers could have on the other departments in which they teach.

It is perhaps appropriate at this point to examine some of the problems encountered in trying to involve teachers in such reflective exercises or even to maintain those exercises that are taking place. The energy required to sustain such involvement may be as great or even greater than that required to initiate it. This provides enormous problems in providing necessary support and motivation. Altruism is a motive played on by many curriculum developers in an effort to involve and support teachers. I am sure that in practice its role is less than is assumed. It is interesting to note that as part of various research projects many small groups, after producing excellent self reflective reports, disband themselves on completion. The motivation was in producing a report document rather than in connection with self development.

Progress has not been easy and it is worth discussing the difficulties encountered if only to illustrate what is required in any serious attempt to help teachers seriously reflect on their own classroom or departmental practice. 'Why get involved?' is a question rarely asked or answered. But it should be asked of all those staff whom one wishes to involve and particularly of those who, by their status with their colleagues, would be in an ideal position to provide the support required. Such people can be regarded as the key to success and little can be done in the area of self development, on anything but a small scale, without their sympathetic support. In secondary schools, for example, such people could be the Heads of Department. Without their support it may be desirable, if all attempts at influencing fail, to wait for, or even pray for, the resignation of such people. The person appointed as the replacement may be sympathetic to self development and will certainly not be initially threatening.

So, why should anyone want to get involved? Or should I rather ask, Why should we *not* get involved?

1. *Does it matter if one does not operate as an effective teacher?*
   It need not.
      Why spend time and effort in doing something if no-one cares or even knows whether you have done it? In some instances it is even possible to retreat into a classroom and give the illusion of being an effective teacher. How many teachers get rewarded for saying what they do rather than doing what they say?
      If there is no way that our efforts can be identified and there is nothing to make it worth doing, it will tend not to get done. Schools must therefore be adept at recognising and rewarding staff who demonstrate the skills that they feel will be of value to the pupils.

2. *Is it difficult to be an effective teacher?*
   Yes: the accumulation of problems identified within a department or an individual may demonstrate incompetence in colleagues' eyes or in the eyes of the hierarchy.

Yes: in-service training is often regarded as remedial treatment making up for deficiencies.

Yes: by all means get involved, but you will have to spend a significant amount of time doing it, and, by the way, doing it in your own time.

Yes: I don't mind giving up time, but if I want promotion I shall have to demonstrate my administrative skills rather than my teaching skills. In many schools financial structures and promotion have little direct relationship to improvement of teaching performance. To be promoted one often has to demonstrate non-teaching skills.

Yes: self monitoring threatens a teacher's self esteem and feelings of professional confidence. S/he sees his or herself as s/he is, rather than s/he thought s/he was. S/he sees his or her classroom as a collection of complex interactions that s/he does not fully understand.

People soon learn to avoid those things that cause problems. Self evaluation is an intellectually demanding and onerous task whose success depends on the development of quite substantial support systems, and on including some serious thought given to the problems of motivation. No school can embark upon any large-scale exercise involving self evaluation without thoroughly preparing the ground in this respect. The success of such large-scale staff involvement in a school is thus going to be very much dependent on some key figures in the movement being in a position of power.

What can be done about the increased teacher workload? Teachers will find themselves spending considerably more time than usual. To what extent can we safeguard free time for staff involvement? Can meetings be accommodated in the school day? Can we use spare time created by upper school children leaving after examinations? What burdens can be removed that are presently regarded as acceptable requirements of the school bureaucracy?

What can a school do about increasing the awareness of

inadequacies? Often the hierarchy within a school is concerned not so much with developing those capabilities which help teachers in the classroom, but with apportioning praise and blame and thereby calling teachers to account. A hierarchy should be fully supportive of its staff and regard self development and criticism as being a sign of strength which is recognised and rewarded. To set an example, the hierarchy itself should also be involved in such reflective activities.

What can a school do in terms of its resources? Schools should make readily available those items of hardware and software that could be of support to individuals and groups. Advisers such as external speakers, members of the advisory team and HMIs should be available and should be seen to be both sympathetic and supportive. What can a school do about providing motivation for staff? This is probably the most difficult and yet most important question to answer. In view of our present falling rolls little can be done in providing financial rewards or promotion. Much more can be done in developing an organisation that would enable any hierarchy to recognise and praise such staff involvement.

To develop an elaborate support structure thus requires answers for many questions. It is apparent that at least one member of the self evaluation movement should be a person with sufficient power not only to ask these questions but also to influence those capable of making the relevant decisions. Certain conditions within a school can easily inhibit a teacher's professional development. Removal of these conditions, however, will only provide the environment in which development may take place. Changing the conditions may therefore facilitate staff involvement, but they will not ensure it. Setting up an effective support structure should thus be seen as a prerequisite for large-scale staff involvement, but not necessarily the catalyst for initiating such involvement.

So who or what should the catalyst be? Probably those individuals or individual who had the influence with the hierarchy in setting up a support structure. They must, however, be people who are seen as being sympathetic to the needs of teachers, respected by the staff and above all people who are not regarded as critical informers for the hierarchy. Such people are required to seize upon those opportunities that may present themselves, in order to introduce and develop the concept of self evaluation. They must be people who by their enthusiasm and recognition can provide constructive support and thus some of the motivation required in any long-term evaluation exercise. As I have already indicated, the task will be simplified if we are dealing with staff who find themselves in a new situation and thus more able to accept change, such as in the development of new courses or in the appointment of new staff. It has been relatively easy in such situations for interested staff to be that catalyst. Such situations are often self perpetuating. Staff involved in our MACOS team have in the past seized upon the opportunities developing in other areas of the curriculum in which they teach, recognising a change in conditions which has allowed them to sow the seeds of self evaluation.

So much for making the best use of the opportunities that arise, but how can those staff who still find such exercises too threatening or time-consuming be encouraged to take part? I have been involved in such an experiment for a number of years. Initially all staff and departments were required to take part in a highly structured exercise of formulating, in a very traditional objective fashion, the path along which they were travelling. Such an exercise in my view could provide a talking point, and a foundation for the development of criteria for evaluation. The school has provided the opportunity for all staff to be involved in a debate on the needs of our pupils and then to formulate by common agreement a new curriculum and organisational structure to be implemented for the remainder of the 1980s. Such an opportunity has demonstrated the willingness of the hierarchy to be as self reflective as anyone else, even to be seen as targets. As Co-ordinator for In-Service Training I am part of the support structure and have been invited to the vast majority of departmental and inter-departmental discussions that have taken place in connection with this task. Any recommendations or suggestions eventually made will, of course, have to be substantiated by some form of evidence. Departments are thus becoming increasingly involved in visiting other schools and educational institutes bringing into the school external speakers and advisers and thus gradually developing the confidence required to enable as many staff as possible to become self critical and reflective problem solvers. The catalyst in this experiment is the hierarchy itself. The management team is increasingly being perceived as a sympathetic team of equal partners working within and amongst departments, rather than administrators who occasionally teach. With continuous involvement such members of the management team will be able to take part, advise, recognise, praise and be seen to be developing themselves. By employing such an approach and in taking advantage of those opportunities that arise I am hoping that, given time, a greater number of individuals and departments can be involved in such work. A common criticism of forms of school-based evaluation is that they are often biased or crude and thus invalid and unreliable. At the same time as increasing the number of staff who are getting involved in self evaluation work we are therefore attempting to increase the range of techniques that we employ and thus increase the range of perspectives available. Those currently in use include the identification of recurring patterns in lesson transcripts, the triangulation methods as developed in the Ford Teaching Project, various observation check lists and more traditional tests designed to identify the acquisition of various skills and concepts. In some areas of the school we are attempting to obtain outside perspectives of departments, initially from colleagues in other departments. In the near future we are hoping to bring in people from outside the school to make their own evaluation. In two particular areas we have been experimenting in obtaining and using the perspectives of our own pupils. In one department children have been required to answer fifty questions concerning their own classroom environment. In the other department children are provided with forms which can be completed anonymously and include any comment or statement the children wish to make at the conclusion of each five-week section of work.

In becoming increasingly aware of our own individual performance and of those complicated interactions that take place in the classroom, we are becoming increasingly accountable to ourselves. The more accountable we are to ourselves the more accountable we will be to any outside agency whether it be the DES, LEA, or parents. If we know what we are doing and why, then we should be able to justify ourselves. As a spin-off, an outside evaluator could provide that stamp of approval for the school's own evaluation. The outsider's evaluation together with the teacher's evaluation could stand side by side as the school's evaluation audit available for inspection by the community. I would certainly like to see the staff at our school develop sufficient confidence, over the next two or three years, in their ability as self evaluators to 'go public' with full community involvement.

JON NIXON

Pointers: 2

* The studies in this section have outlined some of the ways in which teachers can support one another in implementing action research. Those wishing to explore this theme in more detail might well turn to the teachers' case studies that are included in *School-Based Curriculum Development in Britain* (see Appendix).

* Informal talk about pupils, about what has happened in a particular lesson and about one's own teaching is an important part of every teacher's professional development. Classroom observation is one way of enriching this talk and giving it focus.

* A vital issue in action research concerns the control of data. When pupils are involved in the research this issue may become particularly problematic. In schools where action research is being carried out procedures for the clearance of data need to be clearly understood by all parties.

* School-based research is more likely to prove effective when developed by a group of teachers rather than by an individual. Ideally such a group would be cross-curricular and would include teachers of differing status within the school hierarchy.

* Designing a questionnaire requires the clear formulation of questions and a precise use of language. A useful model for questionnaire design and analysis can be found in the Ford Teaching project booklet, *Team Based Action Research* (see Appendix).

* A starting point for whole school evaluation is the formulation of a checklist which is agreed on by all the staff. An example of such a checklist can be found on pages 132–138 of *Evaluation and the Teacher's Role* (see Appendix).

3

Looking outside

JON NIXON

Looking outside

How can those working in classrooms and those outside schools co-operate on the emergence of a research tradition which will benefit teaching? In addressing themselves to this question the authors of the first three chapters in this section outline some of the ways in which outside agencies can support action research. Teachers' Centres, institutions of higher education and curriculum research and development projects are shown as having a potentially vital part to play in facilitating teacher initiated research. But teachers, it must be remembered, have much to offer in return. For, as the final chapter of this guide makes clear, their contribution to knowledge about schooling is unique. Teachers, pupils, administrators, academics and policy makers could all benefit from reading or hearing about research done by teachers. This section presents only a small number of the supportive frameworks available. A more representative sample is included in the appendix which lists co-ordinating networks and publications catering specifically for teachers involved in classroom research.

The frameworks in existence are a response to three main areas of need: for information about alternative research methods, for co-ordination of the work of individual teacher researchers, and for effective dissemination.

1. One of the blocks to the development of action research in schools is the lack of information concerning the range of research techniques available for use in the classroom. Many teachers, if they think of educational research at all, see it within a narrow tradition of psychometric testing and statistical analysis. It is hardly surprising, therefore, that they consider its relevance to their own concerns as

distinctly limited. Outside agencies could provide a useful service by offering advice and information on alternative research techniques.

2. The need for co-ordination is particularly urgent within
   certain geographical areas and subject specialisms. A
   teacher working in a large department is likely to feel much
   less isolated than someone who is in a department of one or
   two. Similarly, in rural areas where schools may be a
   considerable distance apart the problem of putting teachers
   with similar research interests in touch with one another is
   particularly pressing. Institutions situated outside the
   school have a vital role to play in the co-ordination of
   isolated initiatives; not only as impersonal clearing houses,
   but as supportive frameworks which sustain and encourage
   collaborative research.

3. Dissemination is a crucial part of the research process.
   Within the school dissemination should be gradually
   broadened to include pupils and parents. Local education
   authorities can further facilitate the flow of ideas by creating opportunities for teachers of different age groups and
   subject specialisms to share their research interests across a
   community of schools. At the national level the networks
   mentioned in the apendix serve a valuable function. For
   dissemination to be effective it must be seen as integral to
   the research design, not as an optional extra tagged on the
   end.

RAY SHOSTAK

Teachers' centres

Writing anything about the relationship between teachers and teachers' centres is a terrible risk. One is often faced with the criticism 'but my local centre isn't like that'. For some this will be true simply because there are many different institutions each *called* teachers' centres. But there are now a number of centres scattered throughout the country which have developed according to similar principles. These have not only a fundamental commitment to working with classroom teachers in context, but also a most specific commitment to supporting teachers both as individuals, and in groups, who wish to work in areas such as school-based research. In such centres 'teacher as researcher' activities will be seen in a variety of formats as they compete for priority with the many interests of teachers, wardens and other educators. Experience now shows that centres can, and do, help teachers to help themselves in their work. What follows is an attempt to illustrate some of the ways that centres can do this by exploring three major themes of support: (a) by maximising and providing educational expertise; (b) by maximising and providing resources (human, material and financial); and (c) by facilitating discussion and sharing of ideas and thinking. Before turning to these three themes it is important first that we all agree what it is we mean when we make reference to teachers' centres; and secondly to explore exactly what the teacher's role is in relation to such an institution. From this introduction, albeit brief, I hope will emerge a sense of the local centre's potential for helping individual teachers in their work.

I will begin by stating that a teachers' centre is a long term contract between a local education authority and its teachers to create opportunities, in context, which will lead to the development of teachers and the curriculum and therefore an improvement in classroom practice. This is made possible as a consequence of the actions of the three major constituents: support from the local education authority, commitment by centre staff, and the professionalism (and the commitment that implies) of teachers. The local education authority must ensure that a centre has suitable resources; the centre staff must be able to create systems which allow teachers to communicate efficiently and accurately with the centre's decision-making groups (and then are capable of making things happen!); and, most importantly, the teachers must influence decision making and ensure that the centre meets their needs. Should any of these elements be deficient the centre will have difficulty in fulfilling the definition and it must be remembered that the teachers can, and must, influence the others to make it theirs.

Centres have now been in existence long enough to begin the analysis of their operations through the three elements noted above. It is true that unless the LEA has played its part in providing appropriate resources the centre would be a non-starter; and it is also true that unless centre staff are committed to 'making things happen' the job of a teacher is that much more difficult; but although such a centre is a partnership, it is the teachers who inevitably turn the concept into reality. For unless teachers do accept their full responsibilities towards professional and curricular growth, then what has been called a teachers' centre will never be anything other than a centre for teachers. One can, therefore, look at the partnership in action and assess which elements have succeeded in working towards the creation of opportunities for teachers and, indeed, whether teachers have accepted their responsibilities for the centre.

A teacher's responsibility towards his or her centre is two-fold: first, to participate in expressing wants and needs regarding professional and curricular development; and, second, to contribute experience and expertise to others. An individual's experiences are both a starting point for his own development and also of value for others to reflect upon. In centres, classroom teachers (both primary and secondary), administrators and college lecturers all come together to learn from the sharing and exploring of their work, its context, method and philosophy.

The local nature of centres gives the perfect non-authoritarian, secure environment for this. Through the opportunities created will come a clear and more consistent educational service.

Each centre will naturally vary in the structures it creates for identifying areas for questioning and in its modes of provision of appropriate activities. At the South West Hertfordshire Centre, for example, there are three major decision making structures for future centre-based activities: the correspondents' group, a number of content-based planning groups, and the centre staff themselves (there is, of course, some overlap between them). All three structures for decision-making are fed with ideas by individual teachers and new activities begin with classroom practice rather than educational theory. It is worth noting that although the centre is educationally accountable through the correspondents' group (thereby to the teachers in individual schools) the demand has grown beyond the centre's ability to respond immediately to all requests. We continually re-evaluate our policy priorities through an elected group of teachers called the 'Working Committee'.

In practice the majority of the centre's programme is directed by the correspondents' group which meets twice a term to evaluate past activities, and consider ideas for future work and general centre development. Each correspondent has a small enough constituency (his or her own school) in which real information and views can be communicated. The group has built up a very close relationship with centre staff, and with each other, and now can express accurately the demands of their staff. Centre staff, advisers, schools and individual teachers all contribute to the correspondents' group; the outcomes of the discussions will be a decision either to mount an activity or to refer it back to school for further refinement and discussion.

The content planning groups are made up of interested teachers who want to look at a specific area of education (such as language development, mathematics, the use of audio-visual aids, or religious education). The groups plan activities to meet their own needs. These same activities are offered to other interested teachers in the division. The intention, however, is that the groups should plan for themselves. Often ideas from other sources are fed to the planning groups for comment and, once again, individual teachers have direct access to the decision-making on centre activities.

The third decision-making group at the centre consists of the centre staff themselves. Teachers bring ideas for activities to us directly either on visits to the centre or when we are out in schools. If there is any doubt about interest the idea can be referred to either of the previous two structures. But since we are just as concerned with individual needs as we are with group needs, often ideas for new activities can come from one of us or from an individual teacher noting his concern with a particular topic.

Once areas for work have been identified it is normally centre staff (through consultation and negotiation with teachers) who identify the appropriate expertise and design suitable activities. Together with teachers, the centre creates opportunities relating to the interests of the locality. The examples of work which follow have involved both primary and secondary school teachers. They illustrate one centre's response when individuals, or small groups, expressed interest in particular issues. They are not intended to be an exhaustive survey in terms of the ways centres work with teachers on school-based research, but rather to illustrate some of the models used in responding to the particular areas of enquiry which teachers wish to explore.

'Rules' for the teacher as researcher have not yet been written. Often teachers are engaged in research activities and either do not recognise the fact or do not wish to have it compared with the traditional idea of educational research. There are also others who wish to involve themselves in a more formal research procedure but are uncertain of the skills required. It is for both these groups of teachers that the centre can often mount activities that will encourage teacher development by matching those who are interested with others who have had experience related to the particular topic, or are doing some research themselves into the area of concern.

The first example illustrates the centre's role in this matching of expertise to teachers' needs. Interest was stimulated in school-based research after a conference for local primary headteachers was held at the centre on 'The Interrelationship of Pupil Learning, Teacher Performance and School Evaluation'. The conference was the first of the headteachers' annual three-day conferences mounted by the centre under the direction and control of a planning group of primary heads (an evaluation report is available from the centre). As one of the outcomes of the conference a number of local heads and teachers began to involve themselves in more formal investigations within their schools. Many were particularly interested in looking at the questioning techniques they used with children, both within their classrooms and in more informal chats. With this in mind the centre mounted a series of day conferences (with follow-up support) to explore techniques and issues relating to teacher research in general and questioning in particular. The first was called 'Ways of Doing Research' and it covered the various ways in which a classroom teacher could organise more formal enquiries within his or her own classroom. It was a practical day looking at using tape recorders, conducting multiple interviews, interviewing pupils and writing questionnaires and field notes.

The second day conference was entitled 'Questioning Strategies', and its main aim was for the participants to examine the following issues:

> What sort of questions are you asking?
> Do they encourage pupils to think or do they interfere with their thought processes?
> Do they give the answer in the questions?
> What are you giving away non-verbally?

Both conferences lasted a day and were led by a lecturer from a local Institute of Education. Both involved practising particular techniques and the sharing of experiences and expertise.

From both conferences it emerged that teachers were either individually, or with other members of their respectives staffs, in small groups, researching issues within their classrooms (two accounts of this work appear in *CARN Bulletin 2*, see Appendix). The point of this example is that, starting from the interests of teachers, the centre was able to locate someone with appropriate expertise and, more importantly, able to organise that person to come and work with the teachers. There was no expert giving the answers, instead someone with experience of work in this particular educational area was made available to work with the teachers. Additionally, the centre gave support, both material and human, for the school-based research that was started. All centres will have access to limited funds for these purposes, should they find a particular need in their locality. More important than finding the expertise is identifying the need; as long as the centre hears the teacher clearly the rest is relatively simple.

One of the unique features of centres' work is that they can normally respond to a teacher's request swiftly, as there is minimum of red tape. The staff can link up with a variety of different networks, and the first to be considered with most requests concerning teacher research, are local teachers themselves. Who better to work with a teacher than someone who has undergone the process of doing research while teaching and knows the problems first hand? Wardens will, therefore, spend considerable time in schools and at the centre talking to teachers, discovering their individual interests and skills. If there is no one locally, however (as was the case in the example above), then wider networks will be explored. These will include staff at educational institutes, colleges or universities, Schools Council staff, or even other wardens who may know a suitable teacher in their catchment area. What is crucial to the process is the realisation that seeking help is not a sign of failure but a sign of interest and part of our professional commitment as teachers.

The second example concerns resources. This can best be seen by focusing on a centre activity in which individual teachers began to research various aspects of their schools, under the title of 'evaluation'. The opportunity was created for teachers who were interested in any, or all, of the following areas: (1) systematically evaluating their existing learning and teaching programmes as a basis for developing materials and strategies; (2) assessing both published and home-made materials and the contribution they make to learning; (3) gaining an understanding of the methods of assessment open to teachers; and (4) beginning to do 'action research' within schools.

It became clear that, although each individual would be looking at different issues, their experiences and thinking would be helpful to others in designing their work; and that teachers could develop into a support group. So they did begin to get together to talk about areas in which they wished to study. At times the group would have an outside consultant in (which the centre could arrange), at times they just shared their problems in doing the work. This was not a course in the traditional sense, but an opportunity, supported by the centre, which enabled teachers to work together and grow in educational understanding.

Over the first term eleven teachers met on five occasions. For each meeting they individually prepared proposals and the group discussed them and explored the various educational and research aspects of each. The discussions were wide-ranging, enabling individuals to translate ideas into their own thinking. Although not every teacher began with a focus, through the term each identified an area in which they would continue to research. The resources demand of the teachers was wide and varied during this defining stage.

One of the first resources to be used was the centre's professional library. This is a loan collection of some twelve thousand books relating to educational theory and practice. The titles borrowed by the group ranged from the content specific (language development) to the more general (child development). If books were not in the library, then recourse to the Hertfordshire Library Service was always possible. When considering published material, however, it must be remembered that there is often a substantial time delay between a book being written and its publication. Additionally, there are many who would write an article about work they are doing and never write a book. Recognising this, and that much research is published initially in report form, the centre also subscribes to a large number of periodicals and journals. Centre staff scan these periodicals for relevant articles and, at the same time, keep an eye out for the less publicised pamphlets and special reports that are often produced by research groups, education organisations and higher education establishments. If any are thought to be useful for the teachers the centre is working with then one is bought for display, sets are bought for particular groups, and sometimes the centre buys in bulk for general resale to teachers. Examples of such useful publications include the Ford T material (Cambridge Institute of Education, see Appendix), Rediguides: Guides in Education Research (University of Nottingham[1]), Classroom Action Research Network Bulletins (Cambridge Institute of Education), British Mirrors (Leicester University[2]), many SSRC research project publications, many publications from the Centre for Applied Research in Education at East Anglia, local Authority items and a number of the works available from the Schools Council.

Throughout the Spring and Summer terms, and indeed continuing into the following academic year, many of the teachers began to implement their own research proposals. The group continued to meet and at each meeting one or two of the members would present a progress report for discussion. The supporting role of the group grew through the proposal formulating stage and continued to develop as the real problems of implementing an action research project became apparent. So, too, did their demand for resources increase. As work began, many needed hardware that was not available in schools. This included videotape recorders, cameras, cassette recorders and, the most difficult to obtain, a radio microphone system. Some of the equipment the centre held in its loan collection for teachers, some we had to borrow from other sources (although we did eventually decide to buy a radio microphone ourselves). Additionally, one teacher who was interested in looking at 'children's play' used a triangulation method with the assistance of one of the centre staff. Staff also helped in videotaping lessons and instructing teachers on the use of the equipment. One area where the centre couldn't help, unfortunately, was in transcribing tape recordings. Consequently, we spent some time exploring alternatives with the teachers, including both the collection of information by the teacher using different methods and the collection of similar data by the children and other teachers.

These, of course, are only some of the possible ways in which a centre can provide resources for and support teachers. Each project will have different demands; flexibility and imagination must be the centre's keywords throughout. It is worth mentioning that these teachers are now an additional resource for other teachers; they continue to give to the centre as well as take from it. It is also worth noting that as more teachers involve themselves in research it becomes easier for the centre to meet their resource demands. The centre now has a computer terminal linking into the county computer at the local polytechnic and teachers can learn to use it and book time on it through the centre. Furthermore, we have developed our equipment loan collection and reprographic unit to assist teachers in removing some of the tedium of data processing and dissemination. What is important is that a centre can – and should – develop with the teachers in its catchment area to meet their developing needs. In short, the centre should be developing *with* the teacher.

Finally, the third example illustrates the centre's part in facilitating discussion and the sharing of ideas. Although in both of the previous examples teachers were working on their own projects and sharing their experiences and findings, centres can often help in group-based enquiry or research. In this case, the centre's Language Planning Group offered an opportunity for teachers to work together and explore current thinking and approaches to the teaching of listening . . . at least, that is how it started. From a simple feeling of the group that 'children don't listen to teachers now as they used to' a group of teachers found themselves doing significant work within the area of learning to listen. What the centre found was that, after substantial efforts to locate people who could present current thinking, and a major literature search which included the use of the ERIC computer data bank, although everyone thought it was an interesting area for work there had been very little done in this field.

The centre, therefore, created an opportunity for teachers to come together as a group and 'research' the area of listening themselves. This meant that rather than the more traditional 'course' usually mounted by the Language Planning Group (in which the course presents a number of alternatives for teachers to consider and apply to their own experiences and practices) the group presented an 'exploratory exercise'. Having discovered that there were no research findings they could turn to for guidance, they planned an exercise that would enable participants to identify relevant questions and then document their exploration and enquiry into finding answers. The process would be developmental (in the sense that it would be flexible to meet the needs of the group) and it was hoped that it would ultimately reach some conclusions which would help teachers in matching both their practice and the development of materials more closely to children's learning needs. This would be done in a way which would simply be outlined as (a) formulating questions, (b) generating hypotheses, (c) testing hypotheses, and (d) using conclusions to formulate new questions and inform practice.

A very open-ended timetable was put together for the four days which the teachers had committed themselves to attending (two days in succession followed by two more days at weekly intervals). The centre provided each course member with a file of articles which had been obtained in the precourse planning, and the group of fourteen teachers began to define questions and eliminate irrelevant areas of exploration. As we progressed we found ourselves placing the questions we felt worth exploring in more detail into five categories: (1) Why teach listening? (2) How do you teach listening? (3) Are there stages of development? (4) The role of the teacher; and (5) Time spent listening. The implication of each question was studied with regard to child need, teacher action and classroom materials and at the end of the second day teachers returned to classrooms for the intervening week with particular questions to study within their classrooms.

What began to emerge at our next meeting was the existence of a hierarchy of listening skills. In trying to pull the evidence together this list of steps appeared to be the best structure for a further redefinition and application of conclusions to the classroom. So back into the classrooms went the group with their hierarchy and what began to develop was a matrix ('lattice') with listening skills on on side and educational responses (teacher actions or materials) on the other. From this matrix areas could be identified where new materials or teacher responses were missing and then curricular development could be undertaken to create materials in these areas. At the end of the four days teachers returned to schools to continue the field work on listening.

The group has met subsequently on a number of occasions to continue to refine the matrix, share their findings and plan future work. At one stage the work was advanced with the help of three lecturers from a local polytechnic with particular expertise in Kelly's Personal Construct Theory. They introduced the group to Kelly's work and then applied his technique of construct formation and, with the help of a computer analysis programme written by one of the lecturers, looked at our results. This work was also widened and disseminated when the original group asked members of two of the centre's planning groups to test the hierarchy and matrix within their classrooms. Although the work is not completed and although we have not, as yet, pulled all of our data and findings together, we are confident that the work will be a contribution to the thinking in the area of listening development. Indeed in our dissemination so far of the work, we have found great interest in the ideas generated. This dissemination has taken the form of both contributions to countywide courses at a residential centre and also evening lectures at various teachers' centres in the county.

Here again the centre, based on the interests of teachers, was capable of supporting a group of teachers in a more formal enquiry by being able to do some preliminary investigation (both centre staff and those within its network) and by facilitating and documenting the process and findings. By creating the opportunity, providing resources and facilitating the work, the centre has enabled the teachers to question, influence and contribute to current educational thought locally. Moreover, when they reach more definite conclusions and begin to disseminate their work more widely these teachers, working as a group, will contribute to the larger educational debate. They have had additionally the experience of involving themselves in an exciting and valuable in-service exercise.

The three examples quoted are merely illustrations of one teachers' centre's attempts to support teachers as researchers. The opportunities the teachers created (through their centre) demanded in some instances great commitment of time; other opportunities less so. Some of their projects demanded support with human resources, others material. Some demanded traditional approaches to research, others developed new ones. What they all had in common was the desire of classroom teachers to learn, to solve problems and to explore alternatives in a more structured fashion than is normally the case in schools. Additionally, they all took teachers from their individual classrooms into the wider educational perspective with the assistance of their local centre. The ideas came from the teachers; the desire to learn came from the teachers; the support came from the centre. There was a local agency available for teachers to turn to that would create opportunities for teachers as individuals or in groups to explore and develop educational thinking. As part of a network, teachers can link up with the very wide range of knowledge and experience both in their locality and on a much larger scale. Teachers' centres are not only providers of traditional in-service activities: where 'short courses' are appropriate these can be provided. But the options are infinite in both creating and designing learning opportunities. Although we are not completely clear about the part discussion plays in learning, experience clearly indicates that teachers, by exploring their educational ideas and practice with others, may develop themselves as well as contribute to the wider educational debate.

REFERENCES

1. Edited by M. B. Youngman and available from TRC-Rediguides Ltd, 21 Rutland Place, Maidenhead, Berkshire.
2. *British Mirrors: A collection of classroom observation systems*, compiled by Maurice Galton, School of Education, University of Leicester, 1978.

RAY VERRIER

A case for consultancy

Most members of staff working at institutions of higher education are engaged in some form of research as part of their normal
professional lives. In one way or another they are associated with
members of a research community, perhaps as students studying
for a higher degree, or as writers of books or articles on an aspect
of research. They are therefore acquainted with the world of
research; with its methods and procedures for validation, with
its literature, and with others engaged in similar fields of
research. Their professional lives at universities or institutions
of higher education are probably organised in such a way that
they are encouraged with time allocation, resources, study
leave and library facilities to develop and sustain research
interests.

In contrast the lives of most school teachers are not organised
with any expectations that they will even wish to engage in
research. The world of the research community is far away and
headteachers would probably regard a member of staff engaged
in research with more than a shade of suspicion, equating
educational research with an activity of very doubtful relevance
for the school, and as one that draws the teacher away from his
proper role as a teacher.

I intend to consider here some of the ways in which higher
education can assist teachers to do their own research. In
particular I wish to describe how a group of teachers began to
take an interest in action research within their own classrooms,
although the term, action research, is not one they would use to
describe their activities; indeed, it was only later on that any of
the teachers developed an interest in action research.

The consultancy case study I shall examine took place in a
West Sussex middle school. It was initiated by an ex-student of

mine who had been teaching in his present school for three years. Initially the project appeared to the teachers and myself to be concerned with providing the school with the services of a history expert who would make suggestions about the type of teaching and learning resources that could be used by the staff in history. It might be said that the headmaster had perceived a need and had given a task to one member of staff who then sought out assistance to help him tackle the task. My role, as external consultant, was to assist the staff to research history resources, examine and evaluate different types of materials, and offer guidance in making them available to the school. The term, consultant, is gaining currency amongst the providers of school-based in-service. The salient features of a consultancy role, I suggest, are that a voluntary relationship is set up between a professional helper – in this case myself as tutor from a college – and the clients, the headmaster and staff of a school. The relationship was regarded by both parties as temporary. Of particular importance in my relationship with the school was that it was not part of any hierarchical system, as it *may* have been regarded by the teachers if I were a county education adviser or HMI.

I decided to spend the first term talking to all the teachers and pupils, observing history lessons and examining the resources currently used by staff. By the end of the term it became apparent that teachers thought about history teaching in a variety of ways and this influenced their methods and values in teaching the subject. No one set of resources would suit the needs of the whole staff. I therefore proposed that we jointly undertook the teaching of an agreed topic in history during the coming two terms using a range of different types of resources that would be supplied from my college's Curriculum Resources Library, the County Record Office, resource items already in the school, and reference books from the county's School Library Services. In this way teachers could draw upon the types of resources they were accustomed to using as well as having the opportunity to test out resources that were new to them. Each teacher would decide when he wanted to teach the topic and how long it would last. He would also use me in the classroom if and as he considered appropriate. The topic chosen by the staff was Crime and Punishment.

The focus of the project now began to shift slightly towards the classroom use of resources as teachers started, during the following term, to use some of the new types of resource items which had been prepared by myself and a colleague from the County Record Office. The term research was not employed in conversations about the use of the Crime and Punishment kit in class, but a teacher and I in talking about the kit referred to it as 'experimental', meaning that there was no 'correct' sequence in which any of the items should be used, nor that every item had to be used.

This might appear to be a small point of detail, but is an indication of the way in which I hoped the staff would view the new types of resources in the kit. I therefore encouraged them to see the resources as a collection to evaluate and test. These items they considered unsuitable would be changed; items not included, which the teachers felt they needed, could be added; so that finally the school would have several kits on Crime and Punishment to serve the needs of different age groups of pupils and meeting the differing pedagogical requirements of teachers.

The pattern of my involvement with each teacher differed according to the role in which I was cast by them. During this phase of the work, when I was assisting teachers in the classroom, our work tended towards research for personal growth. We were trying to make sense of the resources in class, to reflect on the problems of team teaching, and to gain insights into what was happening to the pupils' understanding of history. The new resources challenged teachers' ideas about the nature of history and the ways in which resource-based learning could be embodied into a school history curriculum. However, before developing some of these ideas, it is necessary to explain teachers' reactions to having an outside consultant with them in class.

My own participation in class had several significant consequences for developing what might be termed the prerequisites for an interest in action research amongst some of the teachers. John Elliott offers a definition of action research that might help clarify the nature of the activity that some teachers moved

towards during the second and third term of the project as they
began to question their own teaching approaches and compare
what they were doing with items from the kit with different
approaches they heard described by their colleagues. Elliott
writes:

> Basically classroom action research relates to any teacher who
> is concerned with his own teaching; the teacher who is
> prepared to question his own approaches in order to improve
> its quality. Therefore the teacher is looking at what is actually
> going on in the classroom. He seeks to improve his own
> understanding of a particular problem rather than impose an
> instant solution upon that problem. Having collected in-
> formation it is crucial that time is taken for thought and
> reflection, although it is implicit in the idea of action research
> that there should be some practical effect or end product to the
> research; but based on an increased awareness of what actually
> happens in the classroom.[1]

I intend to refer to Elliott's action research teacher as a destina-
tion towards which some of the teachers travelled during the
project, rather than as one they had reached already. We need to
know more about the ways in which teachers in school move
towards an action research interest and those factors in the
teacher's motivation and school circumstances that promote this
development.

My participation in a lesson led to conversations about the acts
of teaching. For example, another viewpoint of teaching became
available to a teacher as he observed my lessons, or I observed
his, or if we were engaged in some form of team teaching. At first
conversations were at the level of 'polite table manners', a
necessary stage through which a relationship between a teacher
and outside consultant must pass. Initially I was viewed as the
expert demonstrating how a document should be used in class.
Fortunately all lessons are subject to elements of chance, and
after a few unsuccessful lessons a teacher is quickly aware that
the consultant is not the expert he had imagined. At this stage
the relationship becomes more open and problems can be
explored at a deeper and more significant level. What seems

important about these later conversations between the teacher and consultant is that they promote talk about teaching that is not usually deemed necessary or appropriate amongst colleagues in the staffroom. The shared nature of a teaching experience between teacher and consultant allows for the examination of a common experience which is perceived in different ways by those present. In the staffroom a teacher reporting to a colleague on a lesson has all the evidence at his command and the listener has to accept what he is told. He is not able to say, for example, 'well I noticed that the boys at the back didn't really understand that bit of the lesson', or 'when Mary said that remark I think she was getting at such and such a point that you appeared to miss'. Of course, comments like these could seem threatening to the teacher, and the consultant has to judge the moment when he can offer such observations, and this applies equally to the teacher observer of the consultant's lesson.

For the majority of teachers, working in isolation in their classrooms, this initial experience of sharing lessons seems to be a first step towards establishing a research attitude in their work. Frequently, I discovered, a shared lesson led the teacher and myself towards a next step of agreeing to test out alternative ways of solving a problem in the following lesson. The seeking of alternative possibilities rather than final solutions is a way of delaying answers to a problem in the interest of reflection and further discussion. Sometimes a teacher would test out an alternative teaching strategy in the period of time between my visits and then tell me what had happened. At other times the next history lesson would not take place until my visit the following week. In either case the presence of another interested party encouraged the teacher to take action he may have otherwise forgotten or not considered worthwhile.

I visited the school twice a week during the first and second terms of the project, and once a week during the final summer term. This enabled me to work with most of the teachers in the school for four or five weeks sharing in the same number of half morning or afternoon classroom lessons. In every case it was the teachers who defined my classroom role, sometimes asking me to demonstrate, sometimes to team-teach with a teacher, and, in

one instance, taking half a class on my own to allow a teacher to
try out a new method of working with a smaller number of
pupils. In the latter case the teacher and I took the same
document from the kit as a basis for our work with each group
of pupils.

So far I have indicated some of the prerequisites leading
towards an action research interest by teachers and some ways in
which an outside consultant can assist. How might an initial
interest develop beyond this stage? Drawing upon the project I
intend to sketch the profiles of two teachers with whom I was
working in order to indicate some of the factors which, in these
instances, encouraged or prevented the teacher's emerging interest in action research.

Alan

Alan had been working in the school for about twelve years. He
had been in a Scale 2 post of responsibility and on several
occasions had unsuccessfully applied for promotion in the
school. My early observations and conversations with him
showed that he was entirely satisfied with the history resources
in the school and that he felt he was able to use them in his
teaching in an effective way. He had devised a pattern of project
working which had a specified amount of time allocated to each
topic and a standard outcome for the pupils' work which took
the form of a six or eight page booklet on the topic which was
produced by each pupil. An examination of pupil topic booklets
showed that each followed a similar pattern which included:
some notes copied from the blackboard; a number of short
pieces of writing done by each pupil to a prescribed formula; and
various pages of drawings and illustrations mostly copied from
reference books. In spite of the degree of teacher direction
apparent in these booklets the pupils displayed some pride in
showing them to me: at least that is true of the ones belonging to
the pupils directed over to me by Alan.

When Alan came to tackling the Crime and Punishment topic
he decided that the work must fit his usual method of project
teaching. He expressed interest in my taking one or two sessions
with his class provided they fitted into his scheme of working.

In conversation with me after these sessions he expressed interest in the discussion episodes and seemed keen to draw out the similarities between the ways in which he and I conducted discussion episodes, but he pointed out that I had not done any written work. As our relationship developed in the classroom, and in staffroom encounters, it became clear that Alan was only willing to entertain the use of new teaching resources provided they fitted his tried and tested way of teaching projects. Thus a primary source document, perhaps an eighteenth century Prosecuting Society notice, was presented and treated in class by Alan as if it were a page from a history text or reference book. No attempt was made to help the pupils understand how the document had been produced and its essential quality as a primary source of information. The convention of having a period for 'finished' writing by the end of each lesson directed by Alan, and a predetermined pattern for the use of time in each lesson, were boundary conditions that he was not prepared to change.

Alan's interest in the work his colleagues were doing on the Crime and Punishment topic seemed to be prescribed by the fact that he believed they were working in the same way as he was. Terms like 'discussion', 'pupil investigation', 'creative writing', 'imaginative writing', 'reference work', were frequently used by teachers in telling one another about the nature of the learning activities of their classes. It was possible for teachers like Alan to use these terms to describe what they did with their pupils, although to an observer it was apparent that the enacted reality of the classroom differed from class to class. For example, many teachers talked in the staffroom about pupils' investigating a topic for themselves. The reality I observed in classrooms in this respect varied from pupils finding answers to teachers' questions using books provided for them, to a few classes where pupils were following up a piece of investigation that had been raised by the pupils themselves using a range of sources in the school as well as some books that had been brought to school from home. My own discussion sessions with Alan's pupils must have seemed to him very protracted and disorganised compared with his own procedures for conducting class discussions. He may have viewed my efforts as a poor attempt to use the same discussion techniques as he did, but to far less effect. This raises an important point about observation. It appeared that Alan saw a global activity going on during my lesson which he interpreted as 'doing some discussion', but the fact that each of us was using discussion with a different aim in mind did not apparently strike him as significant. Project learning activities like 'pupil investigation' and 'imaginative writing', used by teachers to tell one another about their pupils' learning, have entered into most teachers' language currency. They are terms that appear to have little more than a vague meaning unless they are related to the purposes and aims that a teacher has in mind when he employs these activities.

Alan's potential development towards a teacher taking an action research approach to his teaching would appear to be blocked by several factors. He had achieved a style of working in the classroom that functioned smoothly and consistently with a minimum of risk because he ensured that the outcomes of all his lessons were predictable. His pupils quickly settled down into a known routine of working that they found safe and comfortable. It might be surmised that if he had been having some problems with his teaching he may have been more open to considering alternative ways of working. It was understandable therefore that he was reluctant to abandon a successful and tried way of working for something that may have appeared to him as new and risky and far less structured. Another feature that characterised Alan and some of his colleagues was the belief that their teaching was the same as that of the rest of the staff. Elliott stresses the disposition of an action research teacher as one who is willing to question his own approaches and look at what is happening in the classroom and this perhaps assumes a teacher who is aware that things about his teaching might be different from what they are. As far as history teaching was concerned Alan felt no unease or disquiet and it is interesting to speculate how far he may have felt some unease or disquiet about a different area of the curriculum, if that had been the focus of my consultancy rather than history. From the beginning of the project Alan had expressed himself as satisfied with the school's history resources and he must have seen my presence in the school as irrelevant. Another possible avenue of influence on Alan might have been through his staff colleagues. Generally he was regarded by them as rather 'set in his ways'. He attended all the staff meetings at which the project was discussed and stoutly maintained that he was doing just the same as they were. They, probably respecting his age and experience, and deeming him to be 'set in his ways', took little interest in showing him that this was not the case. However, the knowledge that any teacher has about the classroom work of colleagues is very limited. From time to time displays of work were mounted in the school for parents' evenings and superficially it can appear that each teacher is working in a similar way because displays of this type do not quickly or easily reveal to a casual observer the type of learning that has led to their production. Whilst some of the teachers engaged in some form of team planning and team executed teaching, Alan chose to work on his own. The clearest indications that teachers in the school possessed about their colleagues came from their new pupils' attitudes to and expectations of learning when they entered their classes at the start of a new academic year. Rightly or wrongly a teacher made judgments about the teacher of the previous year from evidence of this type. Even here the effects of teaching can be masked by blaming shortcomings on the weaknesses of the pupils themselves. One of the most interesting developments that took place during the life of the project was that the Crime and Punishment kit in use provided a common focus for all the staff and opportunities for a more detailed examination of a particular piece of teaching than would normally be available in the school.

David

David had been teaching in the school for four years and was still in the early stages of his teaching career. His main subject had been Art and his classroom bore unmistakable signs of his creative skills with pupils in this area of the curriculum. Unlike Alan, he resisted any temptation to develop a set routine in his teaching. New ideas for presenting topics seemed to come naturally to him and he acknowledged that his main teaching motivation came from working out new ways of presenting and developing topics with his class. In marked contrast to Alan, the length and form of a topic was a response to his pupils' interests. From the start of the in-service project he welcomed the opportunity of engaging in something new and he was the first teacher to begin using the Crime and Punishment kit. David asked me to assist him in a team teaching role by working with half his class on a document whilst he used the same item with the other half. I taped my lessons and left the tape in school for him to listen to, so that on my next visit we could discuss and compare our respective lessons. He had decided that by working with a small group of pupils on the new resources from the kit he could study and observe in more depth the reactions of his pupils.

As a consequence we never saw each other teach because David had decided to use me to reduce the size of his teaching group so that he could test out some of the resources in the kit. In certain respects this had disadvantages for both of us. However, it proved valuable to the extent that it forced each of us to recapture and formulate into words certain essential features of the lessons. The fact that we were working with the same document provided a useful focus of interest and the differences between the lessons deepened our mutual understanding not only of the pupils' responses to the document, but also of the hidden implications and meanings in the document itself. In fact this way of working proved a valuable way of learning about history. In their normal professional lives teachers are seldom required to recount their lessons to someone else in the way in which David and I discussed our teaching. We discovered that, by chance, each of us shared an agreement on the importance we both attached to giving pupils time to make their own meanings, and to formulate and then test their own hypotheses about the document under consideration. This basic similarity of outlook made it immediately easier for us to work together than was the case between Alan and myself. It also held certain problems because of the tendency for each of us to reinforce each other's prejudices. Fortunately, for David, he was able to share his teaching later on with one of my colleagues from the

Institute who became involved in the project and who was able to offer a somewhat different point of view from my own. As a passing observation, it is worth noting that a team consultancy has a number of advantages as it enables more points of view to be generated and alternative groupings between the consultants and teachers.

David's natural disposition as a teacher favoured an open lesson framework that led him easily towards a research attitude in his teaching. He had already done a considerable amount of team teaching with one of his year group colleagues and the presence of another teacher in his classroom presented him with no problems. He was enthusiastic about exploring the teaching problems associated with new curriculum materials and used the opportunity of outside consultants to share his thinking and reflections. Ideally, a teacher like David needs someone with whom he can discuss in order to add depth and challenge to his own perceptions. This type of challenge does not seem possible to obtain in the staffroom, where the conversational norm, in this school, was mainly about forthcoming events in the school, pupils in difficulty, sports matches, and school visits. Although all the staff were present in the staffroom at break times, apart from one on playground duty, the time was usually devoted to rather pressing matters of day to day concern. I found that the most valuable time for talking to teachers was after the school day had ended when it was possible to catch most of the staff for shorter or longer periods of time depending upon their domestic arrangements.

David's experience of team planning and team execution had another useful advantage which was revealed in the way he looked at events in his classroom. He would discuss his lessons from the point of view of his teaching actions and their effects upon the pupils, a way of looking at the classroom that was frequently missing in discussions with other teachers who were more prone to stress the abilities or shortcomings of their pupils. Elliott's description of the action research teacher seems relevant at this point. David's framework of communication about his lessons took account of what was happening in class as a series of shifting relationships between his actions and their effects on the pupils. The presence of an observer, or a teaching partner, encouraged him to develop alternative interpretations of lessons and to test out, in subsequent lessons, alternative strategies. As he was unconcerned about following a predetermined pattern in his teaching, but favoured a more freewheeling approach, he was always willing to test out alternative teaching strategies.

I have attempted to show how two members of staff responded to the Crime and Punishment resources and their attitudes towards taking an action research role to their own teaching. The fact that Alan and David responded in different ways related in part to their teaching philosophy and personality. In the final part of this chapter I wish to draw together a few observations on the school as an institution and its response to this school-based in-service project.

In a small school consisting of members of staff based on one compact campus there was little difficulty in my finding a teacher that I wanted to talk to. The staffroom was regularly used by all members of staff, signs that the teachers in the school enjoyed one another's company and also an indication that this room had become an agreeable and approved area for relaxation as well as the necessary exchange of information relating to the day-to-day concerns of school life. The staffroom had been planned as part of an administration complex which included the school office, the headmaster's room and a resource area of the school. In contrast to a large secondary school I did not have to search out a member of staff from a science prep room or from separate staffrooms.

Dialogues with teachers took place in a number of settings. During the life of the project the school took three occasional day closures to discuss the project: two were held in the school, and one took place at the College where I work. Half a dozen of the normal after-school staff meetings included an item about the project, for which part of the meeting I and my colleague were invited along. Informal chats with individuals took place after school in the staff room and shorter snatches over the lunch table. Throughout my time at the school I kept a case diary in which I noted, amongst other matters, reminders of all conversations, however short they were. The following categories of conversation were all noted down at different points in the diary:

- organisational matters about the timing of projected lessons with teachers
- matters relating to lesson planning and resourcing, in particular notes on items from the Crime and Punishment kit which a teacher thought he might use, and any fears he expressed about using an item
- reviews of lessons that had been shared
- specific conversations about long-term planning for teaching a topic over a number of weeks
- the implications of resource-based learning for a future history scheme
- personal and domestic matters – moving house, the arrival of a baby in a teacher's family, etc
- the future development of the project in the school, and its future after I had left
- accounts of lessons in history that had taken place between my visits
- episodes of teaching that a teacher had shared with my colleague

The majority of the conversations I had took place with an individual teacher or with one or two more joining in, especially after school. Each week I spent half an hour or more with the headmaster who was most willing to set aside time for following the progress of the project. All of these took place in his room and on a few occasions he or I invited along another member of staff or the warden of the local Teachers' Centre. On his visits, the warden also talked with teachers, observed lessons and shared in some of them.

The chance mixture of opportunities in a busy school for periods of quiet reflection between myself and a teacher were limited and often when such an opportunity arose it was interrupted by another teacher who would lead the conversation away to another topic. The categories of conversation given above must not therefore be seen as separate and distinct from one another. It was because of these circumstances that I found the case diary such a useful aid. My notes served as a memory aid enabling me to remind a teacher the following week of a piece of conversation we had the previous week about a teaching idea, a problem that had caused concern, a resource item that was to be tackled in a different way, an interesting idea that a teacher promised to use in a lesson between visits, or a piece of information that the teacher or I promised to provide for the following visit. Brief notes and tape recordings of parts of lessons were sometimes developed by me to provide the teacher with a written account of a shared lesson, or one that had been observed by one of the parties, and offered to him for validation – 'did you see the lesson in this way?' Sometimes a teacher would provide me with notes on a lesson that had been taught between visits, but more often I was given examples of pupils' work as evidence of what had been done. Often this took the form of final draft work although from time to time the more significant first drafts of pieces of work were produced for discussion.

Occasional day closures, when the whole staff sat down together to talk about the project, were often disappointing from the point of view of action research. As indicated above, discussion about the use of resources in class was at far too general a level and phrases like 'we had a discussion together', 'the pupils tested out their ideas with a bit of drama' did little more than give those listening a vague idea of a particular approach that had been used by a teacher. Where these staff discussions proved far more useful was in the discussion of the nature of middle school history and its place in the curriculum. The Crime and Punishment kit had usefully opened up a range of questions about the place of chronology in teaching history, the nature of the discipline, fact and opinion, skills learning and methods of historical investigation, and a much debated area of discussion on the place and nature of written work. Rather like a Pandora's box, the Crime and Punishment kit in use released a wealth of issues and controversies which, before the project, still existed but in a dormant state.

A crucial question in my mind by the end of the consultancy

was how far, and to what extent, teachers could work on some of these issues as researchers. I suspect that the tendency in most schools is to seek a premature closure to controversial issues. There were indications that a number of teachers in some of the year groups wanted to develop new ideas further in the following year and to investigate some of the broader questions that had been raised in discussion about the school's history curriculum. My own plans for the year included some consultancy work of a similar nature in a neighbouring middle school and I promised to retain an 'after care' consultancy role.

It is too soon yet to know how far research issues are being kept alive, or being closed down in the interests of an easy compromise to a difficult problem or because they have been overtaken by other curriculum concerns. From the evidence of several visits to the school since the project finished it is clear that certain staff are working closely together on developing their teaching in history and discussing the outcomes of their lessons in a similar manner to that which I had used with staff during the project. Several changes of 'key' staff in the school have meant that the teachers have had to share the project's thinking with newcomers to the school. This has proved an interesting exercise as it soon became clear that it could not be done simply by giving new teachers a copy of the new history curriculum that was devised at the end of the final term of the project. The new teachers to the school are mostly experienced in their profession with established views of their own and require practical proof that new ideas will work in the classroom. The team teaching structure in the school used for history and geography enables the possibility of the new and established teachers to share thinking in a practical way. The fact that I have been invited to work on a similar project in a neighbouring middle school has made it possible for me not only to visit the project school fairly regularly – several times a term – but also to establish links between a key member of staff from each school.

The project led teachers in the school to engage in reflection and thinking that would help them to make sense of new ways of using learning resources for teaching history. I do not feel that any teacher would have used the term, 'action research' to describe what he or she had been doing. For some teachers the project confirmed in their minds that tried and tested ways of teaching history were correct. It seems very important for a consultant to acknowledge this fact. It was not my object or intention to turn a teacher into a person who would teach history in a particular way although certainly at the start of the project most teachers thought that might be the case, especially when I started working with them in class. Of more importance to me was the fact that every teacher had been placed in a position during the year to review some aspects of teaching. Whilst some became keen and enthusiastic to change quite radically their approach to teaching history, with implications for teaching other areas of the curriculum, others rejected the ideas implicit in using the kit and remained faithful to their pre-project teaching ideas.

The project was initiated because of a need shared by some of the staff, but Alan represents at least one of the teachers who did not see any need for research into resources for history teaching. As explained above, the Crime and Punishment kit in use raised a number of researchable questions that need to be investigated by the school, although they might be assisted in these research tasks by sharing investigations with other schools which are similarly addressing curriculum questions about the place of history in a middle school curriculum.

In this chapter I have attempted to illustrate the role of a consultant in supporting teachers towards becoming resear-chers. By drawing upon a particular case study it has been possible to offer some practical details and implications about the role of higher education in assisting teachers develop action research roles. It is not possible to generalise on ways in which this task can be done, but it is suggested that similar case studies carried out by consultants working in different schools can enable us to build some valid generalisations about the processes involved in promoting teacher – consultancy relationships pro-vided that these efforts do not deny the essentially unique context in which each school operates.

To what extent might it be possible in the future to extend this aspect of an institution of higher education's role in school-based consultancy? Most places of this type are engaged in large programmes of diversification into BA programmes and other types of non-professional course. Thus staffing needs tend to stress the requirements of such courses at the expense of those with good professional teaching experience. For most tutors school-based work is new and a vastly different operation from the more traditional award-bearing in-service course based at an institute. It is true that more of these courses are becoming school-focused (focus far more on the needs of a teacher and the particular school context). In this respect these courses can assist teachers with research procedures and support for carrying out action research in their own schools. However, if these are to be practical and realistic for a teacher and his tutor it seems important that the latter needs to be aware of the school circumstances in which a teacher is working. There is some doubt, frequently expressed, about the isolation of a teacher leaving his school for a course which is not shared or understood by the rest of his colleagues. The school-based consultant is in a position to serve the needs of the whole staff, or at least to keep everyone informed if his work is with the teachers of a year group of one department in a school.

How far, it might be asked, could the role of consultant be done by a county adviser, or HMI? The time requirements of consultancy are unlikely to make it possible for either adviser or HMI to find sufficient time for this role. Indeed, there is some evidence to suggest, at least in a few counties, that advisers do not see consultancy as part of their role. Of more significance perhaps is the fact that a consultant working as a school-based tutor is in no sense in a hierarchical role in relation to teachers. However if he acted both as consultant and tutor to a group of teachers taking an award-bearing course he could be seen by teachers in an assessing role and therefore in a position to influence the outcome of a professional qualification. This need not be an inevitable result of combining two roles – that of school-based consultant and course tutor – but it certainly pre-sents a situation that needs to be considered with care.

REFERENCE

For readers who may be interested in a fuller account of the consultancy role, the author has written a paper for the School of Education, University of Sussex, entitled, 'School-based In-service: A Case Study of School – Consultancy Relationships' (February 1981).

1. Elliott, J., 'Action Research in schools – some guidelines', produced at a conference held at Wolfson Court, Girton College, Cambridge, 7–9 July 1978, Cambridge Institute of Education, p. 1.

DAVID SHEARD

Spreading the message

For an activity that often takes place in full view of twenty or thirty other people, teaching remains a very private thing. Once qualified and declared competent, teachers are inclined to close the door on their colleagues and to frown on any discussion of their performance by those who have witnessed it. A good deal that is made public, in subject journals for instance, may bear only a slight relationship to those illicit and perhaps subversive reports that pupils are inclined to offer, or indeed to the kind of reality that the lone teacher may perceive, amidst the everyday uncertainties and imperfections of the classroom.

Teachers are continually having to respond to unforeseen circumstances, to make judgments about complex and confusing interaction, to make on the spot decisions that will affect subsequent action and outcomes. They often make mistakes, but their access to the mistakes and method of other teachers is as limited as their willingness to make their own experiences in the classroom public.

While there may have been improvements in recent years in the support given to probationary teachers, in the end most teachers still develop their own systems for coping in the classroom with little help from outside their immediate and more intimate colleagues. Whether one judges a particular teacher as successful or not will depend on how success is perceived, but it will owe less than it should to in-service or even to initial training, precisely because any discussion of what is good teaching tends to lack any firm foundation in documented experience.

The kind of evidence of classroom activity dealt with in Part One of this book can provide both a starting point and a continuing impetus to improving performance in the classroom.

For a teacher to describe and reflect on his own practice in some formal and public way, whether that practice is seen as good or bad, may give others not only an insight into alternative systems of coping and a new perspective on their own classrooms. More importantly, it can also help teachers develop ways of assessing and evaluating the effectiveness of their intervention in that fragment of the real world with which they are professionally involved.

But if it was sufficient for some teachers to carry out classroom research, and for others to read about it, the way forward would be clear, and we would already have made some significant strides in the right direction. It is, of course, more difficult to stimulate others with ideas and to modify their action in some way, than to achieve gains from actually carrying out and experiencing action. Those who do action research in the classroom are likely to be more profoundly affected by it than those who read about it. However vivid the report, however significant its meaning, it will not necessarily find an audience that is appropriately wide, or receptive. The real task – beyond the identification of problems and contexts, the development of methodology for classroom action research, and the publication of new ideas and insights – has to do with dissemination and training.

This is not to suggest that reading is not an important means for communicating ideas and stimulating new lines of thought and action, but that teachers may be too deeply immersed in the day-to-day activity of the classroom to spend a significant proportion of their time reading in a responsive and reflective way. They may simply be too busy, even if they have the interest, to maintain the kind of sensitivity to books and journals that is essential to those who continue to work in a more conventionally academic context.

It is revealing that some teachers see as particularly significant to them a period of involvement with one of the range of curriculum projects that have been running in Britain over the last fifteen years. While a project may have been subsequently disappointing in its ability to influence teachers (the take-up of certain curriculum projects has been notoriously poor), actual participation in the trial phase of a project can be the most profound professional experience that a teacher has in the course of a career.

The cynical may explain this in terms of the massive funding and resources that some projects commanded, or the increase in self-esteem accruing from participation in conferences and contact with (sometimes eminent) researchers. Certainly being part of a project is likely to affect teachers simply because it involves a break in the routine, and a sense of contributing to something greater than the frequently frustrating business of teaching their own pupils. But this would not account for the impact that certain styles of dissemination have also had on teachers who could not claim any of the prestige that might be attached to the actual pioneers of new approaches in the classroom.

The Schools Council Humanities Curriculum Project was still influencing teachers well after its 'package' of handbook and materials had been published,[1] not so much through the quality of these publications (indeed teachers very often misunderstood the nature of the project if their contact with it was only through the published materials) as through lengthy, intensive, and frequently stressful training courses. These courses aroused passionate hostility amongst some participants but also a high level of positive involvement from others; they were an attempt to instil the same kind of approach to teaching that would have been generally required of teachers who were collaborating with researchers in curriculum development. This approach demands an increased sensitivity to what is going on in the classroom, and a willingness to monitor the responses of pupils to materials and to different kinds of teacher intervention, to reflect upon and to share with researchers and other teachers the experience of teaching.

The Humanities Curriculum Project made this research-oriented approach the basis of its training courses simply because it regarded self-monitoring as crucial to the success of the teaching style it had developed[2] (discussion of controversial issues with the teacher acting as a neutral chairman). What is interesting is that, according to the reports of some of those who were involved, post-project training had the kind of effect that is more generally felt by those who have actually participated in a project. In other words, their enthusiasm for teaching was increased, they felt they had acquired new skills and a heightened awareness and understanding of what was going on in the classroom. They had gained confidence in themselves as innovators.

What this means is that for educational research to have the maximum impact on those who are concerned with the practice of education, it needs to engage them in an active and practical way. It will not do so if it is presented as a fait accompli, originating in expertise and techniques which are beyond the comprehension of those to whom it is directed. Teachers must be enabled to test hypotheses for themselves in the contexts which are relevant to them; indeed, educational research needs to give teachers the means to continue to research for themselves. Participation will then continue and develop.

What follows concerns one attempt to put these principles into practice, to organise and to disseminate a research project in such a way that it would stimulate teachers to take on a research role. This dissemination was essentially seen as experimental since at all stages the efforts of school-teachers were to be central. While the continuing dissemination of the Schools Council Humanities Curriculum Project is also based on a team of trainers who are mostly working in schools, they are supported by a university-based administrative structure as well as being funded, albeit modestly, by the Schools Council.

The teachers' role in the SSRC/Gulbenkian Foundation Project, 'The Problems and Effects of Teaching About Race Relations', and their work for its dissemination, is not discussed here as any kind of exemplary model. Indeed as an experiment it cannot really be judged a success, but this account is intended to perform some of the functions of reported research as discussed above. It may encourage future dissemination activity that takes account of the experience with which it deals. This is based on my own experience of involvement both with the initiation of the experiment and with a substantial proportion of the subsequent dissemination work, but any judgments it contains owe a substantial debt to the perceptions and insights of a professional researcher who has studied and reported on the efforts of those teachers who have taken part.[3]

The project with which the experiment began[4] sought to document the problems and assess the effects of different styles of teaching about race relations, encompassing an approach in which teacher commitment to improving race relations was made explicit, teaching based on improvised drama, and discussion-based work using the techniques developed by the Humanities Curriculum Project[5] in which the aim was to increase understanding while respecting a diversity of viewpoints to which end the teachers' opinions were withheld.

Teachers in each of the forty sample schools adopted one of these three basic strategies, and arranged to teach the subject to the fourth year (secondary) pupils in the Spring term of 1974, within the context of existing courses. Lawrence Stenhouse who directed the project from the Centre for Applied Research in Education at the University of East Anglia had already worked on the topic of Race with the Humanities Curriculum Project but doubts about the appropriateness of certain types of material and about the 'neutral' strategy had prevented publications of materials in this particular area. He included within the research team a specialist in case-study and a psychologist with extensive experience of measurement work, but the teachers were encouraged and indeed expected to be actively involved in the research by monitoring their own teaching.

The project thus had some of the usual features of applied research: a wide range of cases; its perhaps artificial emphasis on a particular strategy in each classroom; its sampling of a variety of schools (both multiracial and all white); and its study, when possible, of control groups which were not taught about race relations. However, it also stressed the importance of small-scale action research by teachers within their own schools.

This emphasis on classroom action research[2] implied that teachers would collect and record information about what was happening in their classrooms, would share and discuss it where possible with their colleagues and that the development of their teaching strategy would be based on their evaluation of that information. In other words it had to be assumed that any success in the teaching was attributable not only to the basic teaching strategy but also to the action research on which teachers' judgments and decisions were based.

In practice the research content of each teachers' contribution varied considerably and mostly fell short of the ideal of producing comprehensive notes on each lesson, with a specific focus on each pupil and a systematic attempt to unravel and make sense of the intertwined threads of interaction and attitude within the teaching group. But almost all the teachers produced a full set of tape recordings of their lessons, documenting when things went badly wrong as well as where teaching seemed to be successful.

The extensive testing of attitudes that was carried out before and after the teaching term seemed, when results eventually became available, to bear out the feeling that, allowing for deterioration in some cases, as well as striking improvements of attitude in others, inter-ethnic attitudes were generally – though modestly – improved by the teaching.[6] The research as a whole highlighted a wide range of problems and experiences that teachers in this field might learn from and looked in depth at a small sample of classrooms.

But well before this stage was reached, at a conference in the Easter of 1974, it became clear that the participating teachers had found the self-monitoring process to be an experience that had heightened their awareness of and sensibility to their interaction with the pupils. However modest the research attempt, all seemed to find the discipline of reporting on their teaching to other teachers at the final conference to be an illuminating and exciting process by which they were able to learn more about their own teaching.

A modest oral report, given to a small group of teachers in a more formal and systematic way than would normally happen in the staffroom or at a departmental meeting, helped teachers to organise and reflect on their recollections of that classroom experience. By listening and discussing, teachers gained an enlarged view of what they might do in the classroom, and how pupils might respond. Much of what the teachers were able to communicate to each other was anecdotal, but it nevertheless reflected the more systematic observation and record keeping and the deeper analysis that the research role given to teachers by the project had required. They were consequently able to consider different ways of responding to ignorance, apathy, interest, aggression, in the context of teaching about race relations, knowing that what they were hearing was likely to be based on more than just a hazy recollection of what had actually happened.

Teachers participating in large research projects tend to expect to be discarded once their role has been accomplished and the professionals go away to work on the data that have been produced. They work to a different time scale from academic researchers who require an extended period of reflective analysis and writing which does not involve continued close contact with teachers. But in this case the process of sharing experiences and communicating perceptions based on action research led to a strong and powerfully-expressed demand that the partnership with the university-based team continue.[3] The teachers were determined that the process in which they had participated should be continued beyond the requirements of the formal research project; that classroom experiences should be shared with teachers who had not been involved with the project; and that materials to assist in teaching about race relations should be made more widely available. Teachers felt that if the links forged between themselves and the research team went away to their university to work on the data, then this would not be serving the best interests of education.

In part this may be explained by the fact that, as one participant put it, 'dealing with race relations almost necessarily involved certain political considerations'. The university team was seen as an authority that could help to provide 'a driving force . . . to get teaching race relations on the road'. Race had been a more than usually stressful area for teachers and the call for authoritative back-up was understandable and was not in any self conscious or obvious way a consequence of the experience of attempting research in the classroom. However, the teachers who had participated in the project did feel they had gained experience which was in some ways remarkable. As one said 'It's time we stopped hiding our light under a bushel . . . We should start going to teachers' centres and to Local Education Authorities and say "I've got the expertise . . . are you going to use me?" '

It was difficult for the teachers at this stage to clearly identify just what expertise it was that they had to offer. Insofar as the research stance required by the project had become part of their approach to teaching it would have been integral to the unusual and rather special classroom experience that most of them seemed to be conscious of having had. But there was still a feeling that this experience needed to be validated in some way by the professional researchers. 'We are rather hoping,' one speaker said, 'that whatever comes out of the research project from the central team's end is going to represent some kind of authority in helping us to do our job a bit more effectively.' What existed here was a strong conviction that what needed to be disseminated was concerned with good teaching, and should be based on teacher experience, but there was a feeling that this meant providing generalised answers to problems. What many teachers did not realise, perhaps because they remained in some awe of the university team, was that, because every teacher works in a unique situation, in the last resort there can be no universally applicable research findings and no alternative to scrutinising the effects of one's own teaching, in the light of judgments that other people have made about situations that they have examined.

What had emerged from this project then was an intention on the part of participating teachers to embark on some kind of dissemination activity that could make their experience available to others. What they had not defined very clearly was whether their experience was simply teaching in a particularly difficult area or whether what made it special and of value to others was the research stance that it had involved. The fact that all classroom data had been handed over to the university team tended to reinforce the view that dissemination was about teaching strategies, materials, and personal experience because these were what the teachers had retained. But to present these things to an audience of teachers, as one group did in the Autumn of 1974, was unlikely to engage them in the sort of active and practical participation that seemed more likely to affect future action. At this early stage the teachers had no materials available that would enable conference participants to share in and experience for themselves the process of analysing and evaluating what had actually happened in individual lessons.

Some twenty months after the teaching had taken place, transcriptions of some lesson tapes were available to the teachers and it was possible, in January 1976, to convene a conference on the project, mainly for teachers who had participated in the experimental teaching.

Up to this point the university team had maintained communications with the project teachers through a series of bulletins. However, during the two years since the experimental teaching had begun and in the absence of any organisational framework for supporting dissemination, activity had been slight.

There was nevertheless some basis on which to decide that the teachers should bear the brunt of what could be expected to be a growing volume of activity, as some weeks earlier two of the teachers had made a reasonable job of presenting the project to a regional DES conference. So after a briefing on the interim research findings overall responsibility for the project's dissemination was passed to the teachers. It was felt that some central organisation could more effectively co-ordinate the contributions to and organisation of conferences, and since it was expected that royalties from the various publications that would emanate from the project would support its dissemination programme, a properly constituted association which could hold the copyright of materials and a research report, and which was controlled by the project teachers, seemed essential. That the organisation which emerged from the conference in January 1976 was rather grandly called the National Association for Race Relations Teaching and Action Research (NARTAR) seemed justified at the time by the importance of its intended role and the wide geographical location of its membership.

The actual achievement has been more modest. By the end of 1974, NARTAR had contributed to an average of four courses or conferences a year.[3] Contact time ranged from a long weekend to a single lecture, and the volume of work was not sufficient to attract and sustain the membership that had been envisaged. At the same time, the administrative load generated by even this level of activity placed a strain on the teacher-organisers who were too slow to realise that their aim of extended and well-funded courses at a national level was unrealistic in the prevailing economic climate. Perhaps only a local approach through teachers' centres would have given NARTAR the time to recreate the research experience. Controversial elements in the approaches to teaching which were being disseminated were a problem with publishers of educational materials as well as with conference members who wanted some snappy guidance. But despite the inevitable frustrations, teachers welcomed direct contact with school-based disseminators.

In order to build on this initial response the NARTAR teachers had to learn how to structure units of work at conferences, how to chair group discussions, how to lecture to audiences of various sizes and how to work together as a team despite the heterogeneous nature of the teacher group. They were able to achieve a high level of competence in conference planning and management.

In 1979, with the help of a grant from the Gulbenkian Foundation, a handbook was produced entitled 'Teaching About Race Relations'.[7] It contains a varied record of classroom experience, focusing on pupil discussion and documented in a way that requires a reflective and research-oriented approach from the reader. Because it consists of lesson transcripts, edited and classified but without commentary, it illustrated ways in which teachers have worked in this area, and how their pupils have responded, without attempting to impose a particular interpretation on the events. One perhaps unexpected strength of this material is that it documents teaching not simply teaching about race relations. Teachers who study it may learn more about their own teaching by reflecting upon the efforts of others whom they will never meet, and those who do not teach may learn something about classroom realities that would be difficult to capture in any other way.

It may, therefore, be that the work of NARTAR will have made a contribution that is not restricted to the area of teaching about race relations. It is important to remember also that not all the problems that NARTAR has faced had to do with the context of the project from which the Association sprang – indeed the Humanities Curriculum Project has in recent years been looking for an alternative vehicle for dissemination to the extended and costly residential conference and it may be that the attempts of HCP to generate continuing local activity on the basis of one-day conferences holds a solution that NARTAR and other projects with similar needs should consider. Whether teachers will be able to give their energies to self-training sessions in their spare time remains to be seen.

NOTES

1. See 'People in Classrooms', Elliott, J. R., MacDonald, B. (eds), Centre for Applied Research in Education, University of East Anglia 1975.
2. Action research, with specific reference to the Humanities Curriculum Project, is dealt with in Chapter 9 of *Research Methods in Education*, by Cohen and Mannion, Croom Helm, 1980.
3. See Final Report of Social Science Research Council Project HR3483/1, 'A Study in the Dissemination of Action Research' by Jean Rudduck and Lawrence Stenhouse, November 1979. Available from the Centre for Applied Research in Education, University of East Anglia.
4. The design of the project is explained in pages 130–141 of *An Introduction to Curriculum Research and Development* by Lawrence Stenhouse, Heinemann Educational, 1975.
5. For a full explanation of this teaching strategy see *The Humanities Project: An introduction*, Heinemann Educational, 1970; and 'Learning to Teach Through Discussion', ed. Jean Ruddick, Centre for Applied Research in Education, University of East Anglia.
6. For more information see the Final Report of Social Science Research Council Project HR 2001/2 'The Problems and Effects of Teaching About Race Relations' by Lawrence Stenhouse.
7. Patricia J. Sikes (ed.), 'Teaching About Race Relations', National Association for Race Relations Teaching and Action Research, c/o Centre for Applied Research in Education, University of East Anglia, 1979.

GAIL McCUTCHEON

The impact of the insider

For years, as teachers have taught, in one fashion or another they have collected evidence about many matters to improve what has happened in their own classrooms. Whether through in-formal means (such as scanning the room for listless looks and bored faces), or through more formal means (such as administering tests or recording anecdotes), teachers have assessed what transpires in classrooms.

In the 1950s in the United States, Stephen Corey and Abra-ham Shumsky argued for action research, and the term became widely used to refer to research undertaken by teachers. Corey and Shumsky believed teachers' research would lead to an improvement in their own practice. More recently, action research has enjoyed a rebirth. This renewed interest is not apparent only in the United Kingdom, but also in Canada and the United States. What is it about teachers that might render their action research particularly important? The answer is that they are in a unique position to inform others about schooling for two reasons – the nature of their role as teachers, and their presence in school virtually every day.

The teacher's role permits teachers to share a view of practice from the insider's perspective with others – teachers, administra-tors, academics and researchers, policy-makers, and creators of educational resources. The teacher as action researcher can portray his or her own view and put forth interpretations of what happens in a classroom, why that happens, what rules and features of the school affect practice, how a teacher knows when he or she has been successful, how a teacher knows which students need extra help and the form of assistance most likely to be successful for particular students. What does it feel like to be in a classroom as a teacher? What thoughts go through one's head as one teaches a lesson and supervises work? An insider's view is crucial if we are to develop a full understanding of the nature of teaching and the factors that contribute to the making of schools.

Further, the teacher's daily presence in school gives him or her daily access to students, to school life, to colleagues and to his or her own lessons and enables him to carry out long-term studies with a high degree of continuity. In a sense, the teacher is writing the social history of the school. How does learning occur for specific children daily? Does it vary according to subject matter, presentation, grouping, or the medium used? How does the school setting affect what teachers believe they are able to teach, say and do in classrooms? That is, how do administrators' or colleagues' actions and statements affect what teachers conceive of as proper subject matter and ways of acting and teaching in their own classrooms?

Teachers' roles and their continuing presence, then, place them in a unique position to do research. What contributions might their action research make to the educational community at large? That is, how might teachers, administrators, academics, policy-makers, and creators of educational resources benefit from learning of research done by teachers?

Customarily, outsider-researchers have posed the questions, decided how to do the research, carried it out and reported the findings. Many teachers find this process troublesome, for several reasons. For one, outsiders frequently pose questions of little concern to teachers. Teachers are concerned about matters facing them daily, in their particular situations, while outsiders may have other priorities. Further, teachers must act, while outsider-researchers must only provide recommendations as to how others should act. Additionally, teachers or their pupils are 'studied', not 'studiers', and have little or no control over the research, what is reported and how it is disseminated. Having an outsider present, eavesdropping on everything said and watching everything done, may be unsettling when one has no control over what information is collected or how it is made public.

The way in which some research is carried out may also lead

teachers to doubt its merit. Outsiders observing in classrooms for a mere twenty minutes or administering a test on one particular day may cause teachers to question how valid a snapshot of the classroom or of pupils' learning the research actually is; the focus may be too narrow and the glimpse too short to depict a phenomenon adequately. Moreover, reports of research, frequently full of jargon and statistics, are often written in a fashion not easily accessible to teachers. Such research may also be published in hard-to-find journals. Researchers commonly write for other researchers, to acquire jobs, tenure, academic recognition and salary increases, not necessarily to communicate with practitioners. Finally, the tone of much research and many articles is condescending to teachers and negatively critical of them.

A teacher doing action research has the opportunity to pose questions that are relevant to him or her and to seek information that will help the teacher understand his or her own situation more fully. At times, as a result of the research, a different action may be warranted; but at others, no action might be suggested – rather, the teacher-researcher may come to understand some facet of education differently. The teacher's research can lead to an enriched or otherwise changed perception of the classroom.

Such work may also lead to an enhancement of the teacher's feelings of professionalism by being actively involved in a prestigious endeavour, and perhaps by publishing articles or speaking at conferences. The rewards for good teaching and for understanding the nature of the enterprise are few; indeed, they are frequently negative. The 'good' teacher frequently is assigned troublesome students or difficult classes, for, being a 'good' teacher, he or she is thought to be capable of dealing with them. Other good teachers are encouraged to leave teaching, to move into other administrative positions or into academia. Publishing or public speaking may be looked upon as one of the few rewards for teachers who desire to remain in teaching. Those who value good teachers would hope to expand such rewards, and action research may be one way of doing so.

Action research also makes contributions to teachers not engaged in a particular project who read about it in journals or in books such as this. Firstly, the action researcher can serve as a model, demonstrating a larger role of the teacher as problem-solver, active facilitator of understanding, and acquirer of information upon which to base decisions and personal theories about teaching and learning. Secondly, the research report may provide information as to how such a project is undertaken, as well as issues and problems confronted along the way, and, of course, some parts of the research may be generalisable to the reader's own setting. In this case, a teacher reading another's action research might be able to envision how the research can be applied to his or her own setting. For example, Lee Enright's keeping of a journal helped her realise that she had always conceived of the teacher/class relationship as that of performer/audience, and that pupils are more the performers and she as teacher is an audience of one; this realisation may be of value to others. Further, the teacher may gain by having the opportunity to eavesdrop on another. As it stands now, most teachers rarely have the opportunity to observe colleagues at work or to discuss substantive issues with them. Articles reporting action research describing someone else's classroom and someone else's thoughts about a facet of schooling, can at least provide a silent substitute for such discussions.

The profession in general might also profit from action research as the public reads accounts of thoughtful teachers, rather than hearing only reports about the inept and the lazy, as reported occasionally by the media or as alluded to because of declining exam results and other negative publicity.

Action research can go beyond the teaching profession and make a contribution to the work of educational administrators. Quite often, as a result of outsider research, administrators make rules regarding what is to occur in school. For example, recent United States research regarding time-on-task has shown, not surprisingly, that when students spend more time on a particular subject and engage in tasks in which they can be successful with some effort, their achievement increases.[1] As a result, several administrators in the United States have instructed teachers to devote more time to the teaching of reading and mathematics than to other subjects within primary grades. Not only has the research been over-simplified, but teachers are not advised as to the reasons for the ruling. This may be one of the reasons for teacher disenchantment. That is, when teachers who are intimately concerned with the education of the students under their care are removed from the decision-making process and not apprised of the reasons for new rulings, they may develop a sense of futility, seeing themselves as powerless in regard to vital matters.

Action research may help administrators understand that many teachers are higly dedicated professionals, intelligent people who are striving to improve their own teaching and contribute to knowledge about the profession. It may further permit administrators to see salient problems as teachers perceive them. As a result of this increased understanding from the teachers' vantage of the possible effects of decisions on teaching, learning and the curriculum, administrators may be able to introduce supportive policies. Indeed, some of their decisions may be grounded upon teachers' research. For example, one group of teachers is studying the effects of teaching on teachers,[2] work which may have profound implications for administrators concerned about the highly-heralded phenomenon of the under-achieving teacher. They are discovering that when teachers feel over-managed in a bureaucratic system, they may withdraw from genuine interaction with pupils.

To turn to higher education, action research may serve to re-educate academics' perceptions about teachers and the nature of education. A picture of teaching created by the practitioners actually involved in schools could serve to help academics develop a realistic notion of the nature of schools, teaching and teachers. As a result this might transform the nature of courses offered as well as research proposed and communicated. A really productive interchange of ideas could develop between the two groups. Academics might also teach highly relevant teacher training courses, using selections of action research articles.

Perhaps the work of academics can be further supported by teachers as collaborators in research. In a collaborative relationship teacher-researchers and those based in higher education might together make a highly resourceful and valuable team contributing to the knowledge of schooling, for each has different expertise and resources and each is in a different situation. These differences might lend different perspectives to the same research problem, were the relationship truly collaborative in terms of framing the questions, deciding upon methods, gathering information, analysing, interpreting and reporting the findings. For such a relationship to be truly collaborative, the roles and responsibilities of the two researchers would have to be equal, but not necessarily the same. Action research might provide practitioners with the research skills, the esteem within the research community, and the understanding of issues and problems of research necessary for true collaboration to exist.

A further contribution action research could make to academics' work might be by teachers undertaking empirical research replicating other studies or testing theories. For example, Betty Perry[3] became intrigued with Bruner's and Sylva's notion, heard at a conference, that structured nursery activities are more worthwhile than traditional nursery school occupations (such as clay, sand and water play). Bruner and Sylva posited that this was true because children engage in structural activities for longer periods than the traditional activities. When studying this in her nursery school, however, she found that children actually played at the traditional activities for longer periods than educators might believe, given their average attention span. She later went on to question whether duration of an activity is a justifiable criterion for judging the merit of an activity.

Academics' work, then, might be enhanced by action research by its providing them with an understanding from teachers' perspectives of the nature of teaching, with examples of studies for use in teacher training, and with the mutual understanding necessary for teachers and academics to engage in collaborative research. Collaborating on the same topic might permit the educational community to understand a problem as both insiders and outsiders conceive of it and interpret it.

Turning to national policy, government education officers, administrators and legislators frequently make decisions about which rulings should become policy. Should all students follow the same curriculum? Should we move to comprehensive high schools? Are bigger or smaller schools better and, therefore, what should be the enrolment cut-off in schools at different levels? What should the school-leaving age be? What is an optimum class size? They are also frequently concerned with social issues that affect schools, such as the education of pregnant and handicapped students, coping with teenage violence and drug and alcohol use, and how to facilitate ethnic and racial minorities' movement into the mainstream without sacrificing the uniqueness of subcultures.

Decisions about such matters are frequently made, it seems, with little evidence upon which to base them. Action research could be directed toward gathering evidence as well as revealing the influence of such policy decisions. For example, teachers could study the contribution of their particular subject area to multi-ethnic education (as some are), or the differing effects of class size. Such studies might inform decision makers before policies are made, and might also call into question certain policies already in force. The teacher unions, too, and professional organisations might find many such studies useful.

Action research could also influence decision making about the production of educational resources. If these are to be used, then they must obviously be understandable, practical, relatively durable and inexpensive. Research describing how the materials and courses are used, how decisions are made about purchasing them, and documenting what students experience and learn through their use might all help the creators of such resources. Those who produce them may have little understanding of the nature of classrooms. Through action research, information would at least be available to be consulted; as it stands now, little is available written from the perspective of the teacher, the ultimate translator of the resources for students.

Further, studies such as those by David Jackson, Michael Armstrong and David Gower may have implications regarding the structuring and sequencing of learning activities for the classroom. Studies such as Lee Enright's and Alan Root's may help the developers of resources to understand their use or potential use by teachers. The question here, addressed directly or indirectly by such action researchers, regarding how resources are used by teachers and students, might have implications, then, for developers who wish to create more useful materials that would enhance a good education rather than hindering or obstructing it. Studies of the use of resources might also have implications for in-service education regarding implementation of new courses.

Action research, then, has the potential for contributing to the work of many in the educational arena, not only the people mentioned here, and not only in the ways discussed. If education is to be a profession, a host of professionals must strive together to solve the issues and problems within the field. Further, we must do so rather creatively, and learn to talk with one another about the nature of teaching, learning, the curriculum and education, if we are to make decisions, develop teaching strategies and supportive materials, and come to understand the nature of the educational process. Many perspectives and expertise are necessary for this. Action research can have genuine contributions to such endeavours – for a wider audience, as well as for the individual who did the research.

REFERENCES

1. Fisher, C. W., Berliner, D. C., et al., 'Teaching Behaviors, Academic Learning Time, and Student Achievement: An Overview', In C. Denham and A. Lieberman (eds.), *Time to Learn*, Washington, D.C.: National Institute of Education, May 1980, pp. 7–32.
2. Freedman, S., Jackson, J. & Boles, K., 'The Study of the Effects of Teaching on Teachers', paper presented at the American Educational Research Association, Boston, April 1980.
3. Perry, B., 'A Small Scale Observational Project in a Nursery School', Paper delivered at the Conference on the Role of the Teacher in Research, Fircroft College, Birmingham, 16–19 November 1979.

JON NIXON

Pointers: 3

* Terminology is important when communicating with colleagues in other sectors. As well as developing a methodology of classroom enquiry teachers should also be defining at a more theoretical level what they understand by such basic terms as 'research' and 'consultancy'. Lawrence Stenhouse's *An Introduction to Curriculum Research and Development* provides a way in to some of the key issues in the debate (see Appendix).

* The chapter on dissemination included in this section says very little about communication at the local level. Clearly, however, the dissemination of school-based research to colleagues, parents and pupils is of vital importance.

* A research report should be pitched to the needs of its particular audience. Documents distributed within the staff-room often fail to have any impact simply because their authors seem unaware that teachers spend most of their time teaching.

* How might the use of videotape and role-play be developed as a means of disseminating action research?

* A great deal of time has been spent in academic circles discussing whether or not it is possible to derive any meaningful generalisation from specific cases. The relevance of this question to teachers involved in research has been touched on in several articles included in *Classroom Action Research Bulletin Number 4* (see Appendix).

* In action research the function of the 'outsider' is to increase the understanding of the teacher. Decisions concerning the focus of the research should therefore be carefully negotiated.

JON NIXON

Postscript

Between 1964 and 1969 expenditure on educational research and curriculum development in Britain multiplied ten-fold. Though little had been spent previously, this rapid growth in investment raised high hopes concerning the impact of research in schools. Looking back over the last decade these hopes would seem to have remained largely unfulfilled.

Unfortunately, those who hold a stake in educational research have tended to oversimplify the reasons for its lack of impact. On the one hand, teachers have blamed the research community for failing to appreciate the practical nature of their concerns; while, on the other, researchers have blamed the teaching profession for not discerning that the purpose of research is to pose and clarify questions rather than offer solutions. No doubt each side has a point, but the effect of these counter-accusations has been to generate an atmosphere of mutual mistrust, which ultimately can only serve to weaken still further the impact of research in schools.

The real problem is not so much the inadequacy of teachers and researchers, but the inappropriateness of the research model so often applied to education. Imported from the natural sciences, this model is ill-suited to the exploration of individual classrooms. The need for a research tradition which measures qualitatively rather than quantitively, which explores specific instances rather than generalities, and which treats as at least problematical the supposed 'objectivity' of the researcher, is now widely acknowledged. The emergence of such a tradition is only possible, however, if teachers adopt a strong role within the research process.

One of the main points emerging from the work of the teachers represented in this volume is that the contexts which they were seeking to understand were in each case unique. No two classrooms are alike and no two relationships, whether between pupils or pupils and teacher, are identical. For each lesson is a complex web of messages and signals in which the teacher no less than the pupils is inextricably entwined. There can be no single correct way of seeing the classroom; no lens through which the teacher may gaze to achieve a replete image of actuality.

Somehow teachers need to find ways of seeing their class-rooms from new and surprising angles. They need to know how their lessons feel to each of their pupils; how a lesson might feel to an observer, to a colleague who steps into the classroom for a moment. They need to be enabled to transcend the limitations of their own teacherly perspectives, if they are to learn by what fits and starts, by what circuitous routes, their pupils learn.

In spite of the need of teachers to appreciate the complexity of their own classrooms, much teacher education still takes the form of a package deal. Teachers and students are offered courses on 'discussion skills', on 'mixed ability teaching', on 'communication skills in the classroom', as if there were a set of skills that, once acquired, might be applied in any situation. Such an approach to teacher education can only serve to produce dull teachers and inflexible teaching.

A component on the practicalities of action research if in-cluded on all initial teacher education courses, would help to turn the tide. It would also be a way of presenting research as a dynamic process with which the teacher is expected to engage; as a continuing dialogue between theory and classroom practice. Such courses would be staffed by teacher researchers based in schools. Their involvement in initial teacher education courses of this kind would help to create a vital link between teachers engaged in action research and tutors in institutes of higher education.

An introduction to the methods of action research during initial teacher education, although beneficial, would not in itself be sufficient. For a further point that emerges from the preced-ing chapters is that teachers look to action research as a means of developing and modifying a rationale of their own changing practice. In the process of documenting their lessons the teachers held a mirror up to their own practice, to see it reflected in the light of their intentions. That is not to say that their aims were remaining constant. Far from it. The study of what was happening in their classrooms led almost inevitably to a reappraisal of what they felt ought to be happening. Intentions anticipated actions, just as an appraisal of those actions played back upon their intentions. The task of formulating a rationale was a continuing, developing one.

Clearly, opportunities for studying their own work in the classroom should be available to teachers throughout their professional lives. While extremely valuable work in this area can be carried out within the constraints of the normal day, time set aside for planning the research, for interviewing pupils and discussing the findings with other members of staff, is essential if the research is ever to achieve any impact within the school. The education of teachers by teachers into the meaning of their own classrooms should constitute the main thrust of any effective school-focused inservice programme.

In view of this need for the continuing support for teachers in their efforts to develop their own professional expertise, the current tendency among local education authorities to cut spending on education by lopping off provision for inservice education can only be viewed as short-sighted and extremely harmful. Unless funds continue to be directed into both on-site and off-site inservice education the professional standing of teachers will suffer well beyond the turn of the century. Young teachers allowed to extend themselves professionally through the wise provision of inservice resources will be ploughing their expertise back into the profession for the next forty years.

Teachers' centres, institutes of higher education and university departments could play a vital role in showing that school-focused inservice work is a viable and effective enterprise. The enabling work carried out by Ray Shostak and Ray Verrier and described in the previous pages points the way forward to a new style of teacher self-education, whereby practitioners are able to feed off one another's theoretical insights and so achieve new perspectives on their own classrooms. Such efforts must not be allowed to fail through lack of financial backing.

The final point that emerges from the previous chapters is that through their involvement in action research teachers are reaching out to a wider audience, of colleagues in their own and neighbouring schools, of parents and policy makers. The sharing of ideas may be accomplished through staff meetings, through professional journals or through conferences. However it comes about, it represents for the teachers concerned an important element in the action research process. It is a way of exposing their own work to public scrutiny and of learning from the work of others. As such it represents a serious response by teachers to the call for greater professional accountability.

Opportunities for teachers to share their work in this way are, however, limited. Heads are reserved in their enthusiasm for any venture that takes staff out of school. Even given the sympathy of the headteacher and of colleagues, a teacher researcher may find it difficult to find an appropriate forum for his or her particular interest. Yet without such a forum the work that has been undertaken will lack an important dimension and a vital opportunity for professional development will have been missed.

In spite of this clear need among teachers engaged in action research to discuss their work with others similarly involved, the established research community (which could produce just the kind of co-ordinating network necessary), remains, if not entirely closed, at least difficult to penetrate. Individually, many research workers express great enthusiasm for the idea of teachers becoming involved in research. However, the structure of the organisations and institutions within which many professional researchers work is such as to prevent this enthusiasm from finding practical expression.

The Classroom Action Research Network based at the Cambridge Institute of Education (see Appendix) is an exception. It fulfils an extremely useful function in co-ordinating the work of teachers engaged in action research. But it represents only a start. What is required is for every educational research centre to see itself in part as a co-ordinating agency linking the work of individual teacher-researchers or research groups within their area. Research centres could also liaise with each other so as to link the work of teachers across a wider area. Clearly, the Schools Council and the Department of Education & Science have an important contribution to make to this task of co-ordination. What is needed is nothing short of a radical demo-cratisation of the research community.

It is clear, I hope, from the points I have made that action research ought not to be seen as a way of educating teachers on the cheap. On the contrary, if the implications of action research for the professional development of teachers are to be followed through, then initial teacher education would need to be ex-panded, on-site *and* off-site inservice education given greater financial backing and the role of educational research centres extended. Whether or not any of these changes come about will depend largely on how much those who control the purse strings really want a thinking, questioning and enquiring force of teachers.

Appendix I: Networks and reference points

The following lists do not aim at being exhaustive. Inevitably they reflect the interests and concerns of the editor. It is hoped, however, that the publications and networks mentioned in the following pages will provide teachers with some useful contacts in the field of action research.

JOURNALS

Among journals which regularly publish reports of action research undertaken by teachers are:

Cambridge Journal of Education
    Published three times a year by the Cambridge Institute of Education, Shaftesbury Road, Cambridge CB2 2BX.

Classroom Action Research Network Bulletin
    Yearly bulletin published by the Classroom Action Research Network, Cambridge Institute of Education, Shaftesbury Road, Cambridge CB2 2BX.

Curriculum
    Published twice a year by the Association for the Study of the Curriculum, Charlotte Mason College, Ambleside, Cumbria LA22 9BB.

English in Education
    A termly journal published by the National Association for

the Teaching of English, 'Fernleigh', 10b Thornhill Road, Edgerton, Huddersfield HD3 3AU.

Forum: for the discussion of new trends in education
Published three times a year, in September, January and May and available from 11 Pendene Road, Leicester LE2 3DQ.

Remedial Education Journal
Published four times a year by the National Association for Remedial Education, Division and Institute of Education, Arts Tower Floor 9, University of Sheffield S10 2TN.

Schooling and Culture
Termly journal published by the Cultural Studies Department, Inner London Education Authority, Cockpit Arts Workshop, Gateforth Street, London NW8.

The Social Science Teacher
Published four times a year by the Association for the Teaching of the Social Sciences, Stevenage College of Further Education, Monkswood Way, Stevenage, Herts.

Studies in Design Education, Craft and Technology
Published twice a year by Studies in Design and Education, 30 Wenger Crescent, Trentham, Stoke-on-Trent.

Secondary Education Journal
Published three times a year by the National Union of Teachers, Hamilton House, Mabledon Place, London WC1H 9BD.

Teaching Geography
Published four times a year by Longman Group Ltd., Journals Division, 43/45 Annandale Street, Edinburgh EH7 4AT.

The School Science Review
Published by the Association for Science Education, College Lane, Hatfield, Herts AL10 9AA.

Teaching Drama
  Published twice yearly and available from the Drama Department, Moray House College of Education, Holyrood Road, Edinburgh, EH8 8AQ.

NETWORKS

Perhaps the most vital networks are local ones formed by teachers working alongside one another in the classroom. There are, however, a number of national networks which seek to co-ordinate action research on a broader basis.

Association for the Study of the Curriculum (ASC)
  The Association was formally constituted in 1978 by teachers, academics, administrators and others who had regularly attended the annual Standing Conference on Curriculum Studies in different parts of the country. The aim of the Association is to bring together those concerned with, and interested in, curriculum research and policy in all types of institutions. The Association furthers its aim by holding national, regional and local meetings; publishing its journal and other literature; and developing aspects of study and research into curriculum. Much of the country is now covered by regional groups. The Honorary Secretary of the National Council of the Association is Terry Brown, who can be contacted at the University of Durham, School of Education, 48 Old Elvet, Durham DH1 3JH.

British Educational Research Association (BERA)
  Founded in 1975 this association has a membership of almost 450. It has become increasingly concerned with involving teachers more fully in its activities. Its 1978 annual conference held at Leeds included a symposium on the Teacher as Researcher, while current plans include the granting of corporate membership to schools and the sponsoring of regional Saturday conferences which will be of special interest to teachers. Further information is available from the General Secretary, Peter Chambers, Bradford College, Great Horton Road, Bradford BD7 1AY.

Classroom Action Research Network (CARN)

CARN was set up in the wake of the Ford Teaching Project and is co-ordinated by John Elliott who directed the earlier project. Although initially funded by the sales of the Ford T booklets, CARN exists to promote action research in general rather than the Ford T materials in particular. Its bulletin publishes practical and theoretical papers of interest to all those involved in classroom research, while its annual conference concentrates on co-ordinating the work of those involved in action research in schools. CARN has an international membership of over 220 and is based at the Cambridge Institute of Education, Shaftesbury Road, Cambridge CB2 2BX.

National Association for Race Relations Teaching and Action Research (NARTAR)

The background and aims of this association have been outlined in David Sheard's contribution to this volume. NARTAR is based at the Centre for Applied Research in Education, University of East Anglia, Norwich NR4 7TJ.

Schools Council

The Schools Council is anxious to support the work of existing networks as well as to initiate new ones. Schools Council Field Officers often have a detailed knowledge of the curriculum research and development being undertaken in their areas, while *Schools Council Link*, which is published every two months, carries up to date news on work in progress, forthcoming conferences and Schools Council projects. Further information may be obtained from the Schools Council, 160 Great Portland Street, London W1N 6LL.

BOOKS

Ironically, few of the books dealing with the involvement of teachers in research have actually been written by teachers. Most of those listed below have, however, emerged from close collaboration between teachers and those working outside the classroom.

John Elliott and Barry MacDonald, *People in Classrooms*, Occasional Paper No. 2, Centre for Applied Research in Education, University of East Anglia, 1975.

One of the reasons that teacher initiated research has gained momentum over the last two decades has been that a number of curriculum research and development projects have involved teachers, with a view not only to helping define the research problem, but also to implementing research within the classroom context. The Humanities Curriculum Project, based at the Centre for Applied Research in Education, University of East Anglia, and directed by Lawrence Stenhouse, was a forerunner in this style of curriculum research and development, where the project team saw its function as being, in part at least, to create a supportive framework whereby teachers might themselves become researchers. Not surprisingly, therefore, one of the final publications of this particular project took the form of a report by participant teachers. This collection of teachers' essays includes detailed analyses of lessons and also raises more general issues relating to the involvement of teachers in research. It is available from the Centre for Applied Research in Education, University of East Anglia, Norwich NR4 7TJ.

John Eggleston (ed.), *School-Based Curriculum Development in Britain*, Routledge and Kegan Paul, 1980.

This collection of six case studies presents a variety of forms of curriculum development in schools. Each study shows not only the changes that were initiated but also the staffing and administrative implications that arose. There are accounts of school-based developments written by teachers at Codsall, Staffordshire; Manor Park, Newcastle; Abraham Moss Centre, Manchester; and Hele's School, Exeter. There are also studies of the in-school and inter-school activities in the Independent Learning in Science Project and in the Nuffield Integrated Science Project.

Ford Teaching Project, *Unit 1 Patterns of Teaching, Unit 2 Research Methods, Unit 3 Hypotheses, Unit 4 Teacher Case Studies*, Cambridge Institute of Education, Shaftesbury Road, Cambridge CB2 2BX, 1975.

A number of booklets were produced by the Ford Teaching Project (1972–75) which was directed by John Elliott and based at the Centre for Applied Research in Education, University of East Anglia. Working with a group of teachers drawn from a dozen primary and secondary schools in the East Anglia and Cambridgeshire regions, John Elliott and his research officer, Clem Adelman, developed a method of self-monitoring which they termed 'triangulation'. This consisted of techniques for documenting three points of view in the classroom – the pupil's, the teacher's and an observer's – and of procedures for cross-checking the various accounts. The major concern of the project was with the analysis and improvement of the logic and practice of teaching through enquiry and discovery. The booklets are published in four units.

Wynne Harlen (ed.), *Evaluation and the Teacher's Role*, Schools Council Research Studies, Macmillan Education, 1978.

The various chapters of this book, written by different members of the Schools Council evaluators' group, combine to tackle the range of evaluation problems encountered within a school. The early chapters concern the evaluation of individual pupils. Subsequent chapters discuss self-evaluation by the teacher, evaluating organisational and curricular changes and the evaluation of the school as a whole.

Marten Shipman, *In-School Evaluation*, Heinemann Educational, 1979.

Marten Shipman sets out to show how evaluation can be an integral part of the school's total organisation for learning rather than just an optional extra. He is concerned with outlining ways of gathering statistical data; the value of documenting and analysing specific cases of classroom practice is hardly touched upon. Nevertheless, he makes some extremely useful suggestions as to how schools can help themselves by organising their own evaluation of their work.

Lawrence Stenhouse, *An Introduction to Curriculum Research and Development*, Heinemann Educational, 1975.

This book has an extensive coverage of issues and problems relating to curriculum research and development. Although conceived, in part at least, as a text book for use on courses in curriculum and teaching, it also offers a personal view. The linchpin of Stenhouse's theory of curriculum is the idea of 'the teacher as researcher'; an idea that he developed in one of the central chapters of the book.

Rob Walker and Clem Adelman, *A Guide to Classroom Observation*, Methuen, 1975.

Essentially this is a book for student teachers showing how they might research schools and classrooms in ways that make it easier for them to ease themselves into the teaching role. It contains many practical ideas that will also prove useful to the more experienced teacher.

Appendix II: Notes on contributors

Michael Armstrong taught at Countesthorpe College, a Leicestershire Plan Upper School, from 1970 to 1976. For the next three years he taught and carried out research at Sherard County Primary School, Melton Mowbray. He is the author of *Closely Observed Children* (1981). He is now head teacher of Harwell County Primary School, Oxfordshire.

Dave Ebbutt has sixteen years' teaching experience in secondary modern and comprehensive schools in the UK, Nigeria and Uganda. Until recently he was Head of Science in a rural comprehensive where he taught Nuffield Combined Science and Biology. Currently he is Research Fellow at the Cambridge Institute of Education and is working on the Cambridge Accountability Project.

Lee Enright began teaching in a middle school in Dorset in 1974 and in 1977 moved to West Moors Middle School where she is now Second Year Co-ordinator.

David Gower is Head of Science at Hextable School, a mixed comprehensive school in Kent, where he is currently involved in classroom-based research into the ways in which children learn science, as part of a Ph D programme at the University of East Anglia. He is Chief Examiner in Integrated Science for the East Anglia CSE Examinations Board.

David Jackson teaches part-time within the English Department at Toot Hill Comprehensive School, Bingham, Nottinghamshire. He had edited and co-edited several books for use in the classroom.

Mary James has eleven years' experience in secondary modern, grammar and comprehensive schools, where she has taught Religious Education, English and Sociology. Until recently she was Head of Social Studies in a comprehensive school in an outer London borough. Currently she is Research Assistant at the Open University in the Educational Studies faculty.

Gail McCutcheon is an Assistant Professor of Curriculum at Ohio State University in Columbus, Ohio. She taught in elementary schools in various parts of the USA for eight and a half years. Collaborating with teachers, she and colleagues have studied teachers' planning as well as class size and its influence on classroom activity.

Jon Nixon has taught for eight years in comprehensive schools in Hertfordshire and inner London. He is currently Head of the Drama Department at Woodberry Down School, North London, and is carrying out research into the contribution of Drama to multi-ethnic education.

Alan Root has taught in London for nine years, and during that time has taught drama inside an Integrated Studies programme. His interests lie in exploring the use of video in drama, and in continuing research with other teachers.

Nigel Rumble has been teaching science in comprehensive schools for twelve years. He was appointed Head of Science at his present school in 1974 and is now Co-ordinator of In-Service Training. He is a member of Bedfordshire's Advisory Committee for the Provision of In-Service Education.

David Sheard is Head of Humanities at Rossington Comprehensive School in Doncaster. In 1974 he contributed as a classroom teacher and later as a teacher-disseminator to the programme of research into the Problems and Effects of Teaching about Race Relations, which was funded by the SSRC and the Gulbenkian Foundation and based at the Centre for Applied Research in Education, University of East Anglia.

Ray Shostak is Warden of the South West Hertfordshire Teachers' Centre. Before taking up this post he taught in a comprehensive school in Watford and in schools in California.

John Smiddy has taught History in inner London comprehensive schools since 1972. In 1978 he moved from Holland Park School to take up his present post of Head of History at Hackney Downs School.

Ray Verrier taught for sixteen years in primary schools before joining the history department at Bishop Otter College in Chichester in 1971. He has published with John Fines *The Drama of History: an experiment in co-operative teaching*. He is currently engaged as a consultant with several schools as part of the expanding school-based programme of the West Sussex Institute of Higher Education.

Grant McIntyre Limited specialises in social, behavioural and medical science, and publishes books of all kinds – introductory and advanced texts, handbooks and reference works, practical manuals, and important research. Our aim is to make a continuing wealth of new work available to all readers for whom it has value.

Look for our books at your local bookshop, or write for a catalogue or to order direct simply fill in the form below, and list the books you want.

GRANT McINTYRE LIMITED, Sales Office, Bemrose Publishing, 90 Great Russell Street, London WC1B 3PY.

Please send me your latest catalogue/and also/the books on the attached list. I enclose a cheque, postal or money order (no currency) for the purchase price of the books plus 10% (15% for those living outside the UK) to cover postage and packing. (Catalogues and their postage are free.)

NAME *(Block letters please)*:

....

ADDRESS:

....

....

....